Dividend Investing

Expert Advice For Novice Investors:

How To Create A Passive Income Machine And Earn Double-Digit Returns With Proven Dividend Investing Strategies And Simple Analysis Tools

Andrei D. Carlson

Table of Contents

Introduction

The secret wealth machines of the rich are all around us and readily accessible. The problem is people don't know how to access and implement them. In this book, I am going to pull back the curtain as we reveal one of the favorite tools of the rich: *Dividend investing*.

Ever since the concept of stocks was invented, the rich have been using dividends to get paid while they sat at home, traveled, and relaxed. But most everyday people are not even fully aware of how dividends work and how they, too, can build their own passive income stream using dividend-paying stocks.

We're going to explain it to you in plain English, using step-by-step instructions, starting with explaining exactly what dividend stocks are, how to invest in them, and how to use them to build a reliable source of income, whether it's just extra money to supplement your own retirement plan, IRA, or other investments, or if you are looking for a way to live a financially independent life.

Inside, you're going to learn how to do the kind of expert analysis that made people like Warren Buffet super-rich, and how you can create an entirely self-managed plan that will build your wealth over time – provided you stick to it. We'll explore investing in individual companies or using mutual funds and ETFs to build your own dividend-based wealth-producing empire. You'll also learn about unconventional investments that pay dividends, that few outside the ranks of the wealthy even know about.

Dividend investing is easy and accessible. By the time you finish this book, you will know everything that you need to know in order to start building and securing your own financial future.

There are plenty of books on this subject on the market, thanks again for choosing this one! Every effort was made to ensure it is full of as much useful information as possible; please enjoy!

Chapter 1: An Overview of Dividend Stocks

Before we dive into the details, it's important to make sure that all readers clearly understand what dividend stocks are, and why they can be beneficial for investors. In this chapter, we are going to explore the notion of dividends and explain why some stocks pay dividends and some don't. We'll also explore the reasons that investors should be investing, at least in part, in dividend stocks.

What Are Dividends?

Simply put, dividends are a share of profits that are paid out to shareholders. But let's take a step back for a moment and make sure that all readers understand what a shareholder really is. Unfortunately, the general public doesn't get a solid education in finance – if they get any education at all.

A corporation sells ownership stakes or *stock in the company* by issuing shares. This concept was developed in the 17th and 18th centuries, when companies set up for exploration and trade by sea were formed because it got too expensive for individuals to mount expeditions. There were many expenses related to exploration and trade in those days in addition to building ships and getting a crew, including the possibility that a ship could be entirely lost at sea. Since it became too large for an individual or a small number of individuals to gather enough resources to engage in this type of activity, the idea of forming a public corporation was born. This included the concept of selling small shares of ownership to the public in the form of stock.

The company has to distribute its profits to the owners, and this is where the concept of dividends comes from. Dividends are nothing more than a distribution of profits to the shareholders by the company. So, the company takes whatever profit that it is not going to reinvest, divides it up by the total number of shares that have been issued, and then pays out a dividend payment for each share. Today, this typically done on a quarterly basis.

So, a dividend is a proportional share of the company's profits that it has decided not to reinvest.

Do All Stocks Pay Dividends?

The short answer to this question is no. But let's talk about this for a minute so that you can understand why a company will choose to pay dividends or not. It basically comes down to the company's goals as far as growth and market penetration. The age of the company often figures into determining whether or not it is going to pay dividends or not.

A young and rapidly growing company is unlikely to pay dividends. The reason is that the company is looking for rapid growth and penetration into new markets. It is also probably looking to rapidly develop new and competitive products and services. In order to do these things, it needs every last penny it can muster to operate at peak efficiency and meet its goals.

Profits may also be irregular or non-existent when it comes to new and growing companies. For years, Amazon didn't make any profits at all. Companies like Tesla need to invest in building new factories and buying large amounts of raw materials. They also need to invest in hiring many new employees as they ramp up research and development and increase production.

Younger companies tend to be in a rapid growth phase where they are trying to establish themselves in the market. Their revenue and profits are not as secure, and so in many cases, they are not even in a position to pay dividends if they wanted to.

Of course, there are not any hard and fast rules when it comes to business. Apple, for example, is an older company, relatively speaking. When compared to Facebook, Tesla, and Netflix, Apple is a middle-aged man. And not surprisingly, Apple does pay a dividend.

But Apple also invests heavily in R & D, and this has paid off for the company over the past decade or so as they have introduced many game-changing products. So, Apple is an example of a more mature company that is still very innovative and seeking aggressive growth. When you learn about dividends, you'll see that Apple takes a middle ground, paying a dividend, but one that is relatively small. Apple's competitors, like Google, are not paying dividends. They are reinvesting all of their profits, seeking total market domination.

When you look at many mature and well-established companies like IBM and many of the pharmaceutical companies, you'll see that most of them pay dividends, and their dividend payments tend to be higher.

A dividend can make a stock more attractive to investors. In the stock market, investors are seeking appreciation in the stock itself, but if you can get income payments on top of that, it makes the stock a coveted asset. As a result, some companies will attempt to attract investment by offering dividends. Some companies that do this are not in the best shape, so you have to evaluate every company you invest in very carefully rather than just focusing on how much their dividend payment is. If you invest in a company that pays a nice dividend, but it goes bankrupt sometime in the next five years, obviously that is not going to help you lead a financially independent life.

Mature and long-lasting companies are the ones that most dividend investors seek out. These companies have a stable market share, and they also share an important characteristic – they have proven that they are able to weather major economic storms. IBM is a great example of a stable company that pays dividends. It has been around for more than a century and survived massive technological change, the Great Depression, and the recession of 2008. Although the company is not as dominant as it once was, it has also shown the ability to retool itself to adapt to changing environments. In recent decades, IBM has moved from a manufacturer of premier desktop computers to a service-oriented company that has expertise in artificial intelligence and cloud computing. This older company is quintessential for the ideal investment, the stock has appreciated by large amounts over the past 20 years, and the company pays a solid dividend.

To summarize, we can roughly divide corporations into one of four categories when it comes to paying dividends:

- Aggressive Growth: A company seeking aggressive growth is not going to pay dividends at all. Instead, they will reinvest all of their profit back into the company. These stocks typically appreciate rapidly as the company grows and gains more market share.

- Mature but growing: Apple typifies this type of company. It may be an older company, but it is still innovative and seeking aggressive growth. It pays a dividend, but the yield may not be the highest.

- Mature and stable: These are mature companies that are basically stabilized. You can think of older blue-chip companies. They pay regular and reliable dividends. These companies have shown long term market stamina and the ability to weather the largest economic storms.

- Troubled Companies: In this case, a company pays a dividend with a high yield to entice investors into buying the stock.

The age of these companies can vary; it can be an older company struggling to stay alive. Investments in these companies are not necessarily bad investments, but it would take a lot of studies to determine whether or not the company can pull itself out of its current troubles. For most beginning investors, they are best avoided. Watch out for stocks paying high yields that have seen declining share prices. If share prices have dropped significantly, this means that professional and institutional investors have been selling off their holdings in the company.

As we will see in chapter 8, there are also other types of companies that offer dividend like investments. These are specialized investments in areas like real estate, finance, and energy that involve companies that don't have a corporate structure, but they share their profits with investors. As we will see, these offer good and often very lucrative ways to earn dividend income.

Top Things To Look For In A Dividend Stock

Now we have a basic understanding of why companies pay dividends or why they don't. Next, we are going to address some of the issues that you should consider when seeking to invest in dividend-paying stocks.

The first thing to note is the yield. This is the ratio of the annual dividend payment to the share price. In short, the yield gives you a measure that you can compare to other types of investments that would pay interest. In other words, you can look at the yield in order to determine the amount of capital you have to tie up in order to earn the dividend income.

The next thing you'll want to look at is the absolute size of the dividend payment. These are things you need to consider when you are looking at how much income you want to earn each year from dividends. If a dividend pays $2 a year, it might be less attractive than one that pays $6 a year (we are discussing dividend payments on a per-share basis). But there are going to be many factors that you consider when picking a dividend payment.

The stability of the dividend payment is also important, and if the company is 10 years old or older, you are going to want to dig up historical records to determine how the company maintains its dividend payments through a crisis. Fortunately, this information is pretty easy to find. There are many websites that maintain this data, and you can even use free websites like Yahoo Finance and check dividend payments on their stock charts.

A good example is to look at the 2008 financial crisis. Did the company maintain its dividend payments through the crisis? If not, did they restore their dividend payments after the recession was over? Or did they use the recession as an excuse to set a new lower level for their dividends?

If you find a company that keeps its dividends constant or even increases them, during an economic downturn, this is a very good sign. As an exercise, you can compare IBM and Bank of America dividend payments from 2007-2009. Check any company you are thinking of investing in to see how they managed their dividend payments during the financial crisis. Any company that maintained them is a company that values investor relations and looks out for their investors even in bad times. Of course, not all companies are able to do this even if they would like to, but the key here is to find companies that have done so. Remember that IBM also survived the Great Depression.

Generally speaking, you want to seek out companies that show a pattern of increasing dividend payments over the years. This is something that is going to have to be investigated by digging deeper into the company's finances, you want to make sure that the company is increasing dividend payments when it is really able to, and that it's not increasing dividend payments in an effort to attract investors to a bad stock. But if you find that the company has solid financials and it's increasing its dividend payments as the company grows, this is a good investment.

Consistent profits are also important. Remember that dividends are paid for with profits that are left over after the company reinvests in itself. If the company does not have steady profits quarter-to-quarter and over the years, that may be a sign that the company is going to be unable to pay dividends in the future. Professionals advise seeking out investments that show 5-15% earnings growth each year. More than 15% is actually considered a red flag because that is probably not something that is sustainable.

Watch out for large amounts of debt. Sure, a company can use debt when it needs to in order to foster future growth. However, when it comes to dividends, a company with a large amount of debt can be a problem. The reason, of course, is that debt has to be paid back at some point. If a company acquires too much debt, down the road, this could mean that it will have to cut dividend payments or eliminate them entirely in order to pay off its debts. In order to determine whether a company is taking on too much debt, look at the debt to equity ratio. This is the total liabilities divided by the total shareholder equity. Experts typically recommend seeking out companies that have a debt to equity ratio that is less than 2. The lower it is, the better, generally speaking. If the debt to equity ratio is less than 1, then this is a company that is very healthy financially speaking, and if they check off all the other boxes, they can be a good dividend investment.

As an exercise, consider GM. Sure, it's an older company that pays dividends– but GM has many red flags. If you go through our list, you'll probably come to the conclusion that GM is not a company you'd pick for a dividend investment.

The final thing to consider when looking for a good dividend stock is looking at the industry or sector where the company operates. Is the sector a high growth sector that is well-positioned for the future, or is it a stagnant sector that is yesterday's news? Some sectors might be older and mature but have a bright future.

For example, the population is aging. Older people use a lot more healthcare services, and this indicates that any company connected to healthcare could be a good long-term investment. One example is pharmaceutical companies; older people tend to have many more regular prescription drugs that they are taking to manage high blood pressure, high cholesterol, and so forth. More people are going to end up in nursing homes or assisted living as the population continues to age. This means that real estate companies that operate these types of facilities can be good long-term investments as well. But of course, you have to also look at the prospects of government regulation and other factors when considering dividend investments. If Medicare for All were enacted, you might want to research how this is going to impact companies that are involved in providing some type of healthcare-related product or service. Will the company even continue to exist under those circumstances?

It might be an extreme example, but these are among the many things that you need to think about when considering dividend investments. The bottom line with dividend investments is that it is a slow, long-term strategy, and you are not just hoping to profit from the appreciation of the stock

– you're looking to earn a long-term income from it.

Let's sum everything up. The key factors to consider when looking for a dividend stock are:

- Yield
- Dividend payment
- Consistent or increasing dividend payments and yields
- Stable or increasing share price for the stock
- Company stability
- Increasing company earnings with time (5-15% annually)
- Total debt
- Debt to equity ratio
- Industry/Sector prospects

Payout Ratio

The payout ratio is an important quantity that you can look up for any company that pays dividends. I've singled it out because it's so important. This is a direct measure of the ability of the company to continue making dividend payments. If the payout ratio is 80%-100%, that is a big indicator of caution. If it is less than 80%, then this is definitely a good company to invest in.

On the other hand, if the payout ratio is greater than 100%, this is a strong indication that in the future, the company is going to have trouble making dividend payments. A company should not be automatically ruled out because of the payout ratio, but if they have a bad payout ratio, more investigation is going to be necessary before you put your money into that stock.

The Power Of Passive Income

The reason to invest in dividend-paying stocks is that they generate income. If you are investing in stocks that don't pay dividends, when you decide to retire or take income from the stocks, you are going to have to sell the shares in order to generate cash. The beauty of dividend-paying stocks is that you can keep your stock holdings and generate a steady, even lucrative income from the dividend payments. So, you can think of a dividend-paying stock as a 2-for-1 deal.

The earlier and faster you invest in dividend-paying stocks, the sooner you can begin to enjoy a financially independent lifestyle. We aren't going to kid anyone reading this book, getting to the point of enjoying financial independence with dividend-paying stocks is going to take time, patience, and money. But for those who are disciplined investors that are willing to put a consistent plan into action, they will be able to get to a point where they can live lives of complete financial freedom, dependent on no one but themselves.

Why Choose Dividends

The main reason to choose dividend stocks is to build up an income in retirement. Second, when you are investing in dividend stocks you are going beyond the growth found with regular stocks because dividend stocks can be selected that will give you growth that comes with stock market appreciation in addition to the income that they provide, which can be reinvested to grow your portfolio well beyond that.

A dividend investing program can be your entire focus, or you can invest in dividends as a part of a large and diverse investment program. You can do dividend investing independently, which is the main focus of this book, but you can also emphasize dividend investing in your employer managed plans and as a part of an individual retirement account or IRA.

You can also invest in dividend-paying stocks as a part of an investment plan that utilizes other types of investments. It is very compatible with bonds and compliments the overall investment goals that bond investors have but does so while providing access to the high levels of year-over-year growth that only the stock market can provide.

Online Resources

If you are interested in going deep into dividend investing, the top online resource that you can use is dividend.com. This website provides in-depth information about all dividend-paying stocks, exchange-traded funds, mutual funds, as well as giving you information on unconventional investments that provide dividend like payments.

You can also access many free resources like Yahoo Finance, where basic information on any stock is available. This information will also include basic information related to dividends such as the yield and dividend payment.

It is important to be as informed as possible if you are going to be a dividend investor. You don't want to get into a situation where you are investing in bad stocks just because they happen to pay high yields. This is why keeping up with a resource like dividend.com can be very helpful, and you can always consult with financial advisors if you feel like you need outside assistance. Always consult with a professional tax advisor if you are concerned about the tax implications of your dividend investments.

The Ex-Dividend Date

Corporations have certain dates where they record who owns the stock, and there are cutoffs for stock ownership that determine whether or not you will receive a dividend payment. The first date that you need to be aware of is the ex-dividend date. This date is one day before the record date. In order to receive an upcoming dividend payment, you must own the stock by the ex-dividend date. The record date is when your ownership is recorded on the company books for payment.

Dividend payments are normally made in cash, but some companies may pay dividends in the form of additional shares of stock.

Chapter 2: Why Investors Need Dividend Stocks

Generally speaking, there are two ways to approach the stock market. Speculators "trade" stocks and other financial instruments like options, hoping to make short term cash profits. Their goal is to earn money on changing stock prices, but they don't care about the underlying stocks at all.

Whether or not a company is profitable or has good long-term prospects, or what products the company is offering aren't of much relevance to the speculator. They aren't seeking to build wealth for retirement, either; they are seeking to earn profits. Of course, the cash can be used to build wealth, but the point is they are not using investments in the stock market to build long term wealth that they hold for long periods.

Now contrast this with the classic investor. Now we are thinking about a long-term investor that wants to build up a portfolio of stocks that grows with time. The long-term investor may be interested in specific companies that they like, and they may invest in companies that they truly believe in. This is a more traditional type of investing – you put your money in a company hoping that the company is successful and that it grows, over the long term.

Dividend investing follows the second path but takes it a step further. The conventional investor has to sell off their assets in order to generate an income. In contrast, as we mentioned in the first chapter, the dividend investor can keep their assets but still generate an income, often a very substantial one. This is at the heart of the power behind dividend investing to build wealth. And it makes it more sustainable. Someone who has to sell off their assets to get income in retirement has to worry about running out. Do you want to live out your retirement, hoping that you die before your assets run out?

Compound Interest

A key concept when it comes to investing in dividend stocks is compound interest. Most of us have a little familiarity with compound interest. This is a concept that is taught to students in high school algebra classes. But unfortunately, most people forget what they learned in high school algebra, and these days there is very little if any education in basic finance. So, let's quickly review the concept.

Compound interest is a phenomenon that helps a bank account grow exponentially with time. It's based on the fact that money earns more money through interest – and what is the interest? It's more money. So even doing nothing, you have more money in your account with each passing month, and it is earning even more interest. And if you deposit money into the account on a regular basis, that's even more powerful, since the account is going to have two growth engines built in.

Dividend investing works on the same principle. A dividend payment is akin to an interest payment in a bank account. And these days, since interest rates are low, bank accounts and other investment vehicles like bonds have grown less and less attractive. Yields on dividends are at least as good as interest earned in the bank or with bonds, and typically they are higher, often much higher.

An important practice that you should adopt while you are willing and able to work is to reinvest your dividend payments. Doing so will help you grow your account that much faster, and the end result will be that much larger. Reinvesting your dividend payments, which means using them to buy more stock that is usually going to be more shares of the same stock, is the same as keeping your interest income from a bank in the bank account. This is where the compounding comes from.

Let's look at some examples. Suppose that we start with $10,000, and we deposit an additional $500 each month thereafter. We'll assume that we are going to hold this investment for 20 years. Let's also start with a 2% interest rate, compounded annually.

In 20 years, we'll have $160,000.

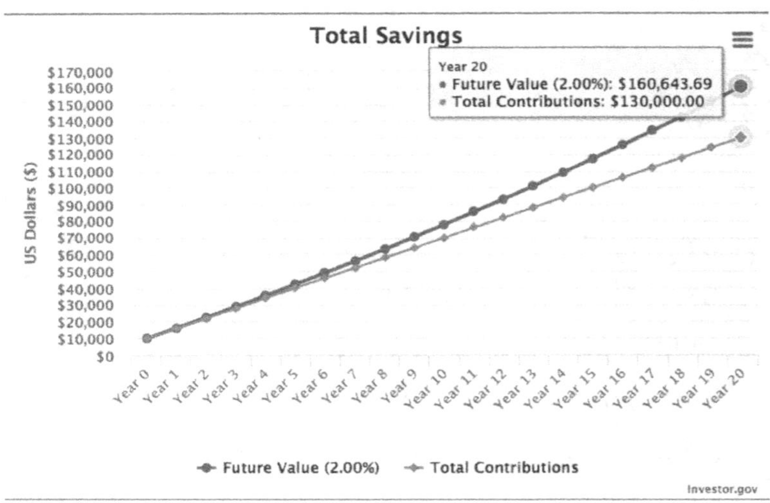

Many dividends pay more than 2%. IBM is currently paying a 4.88% yield. Let's see what changing the interest rate to 4.88% does to our results, leaving everything else unchanged. This simple change has a large impact. Rather than ending up with $160k, we end up with $221k.

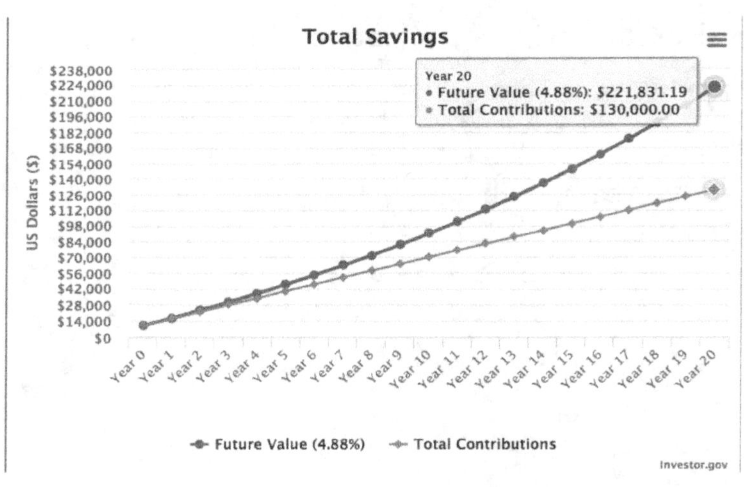

As we'll see, some companies pay even higher yields and there are many "unconventional" investments that pay very high yields. For example, you can invest in energy or real estate trusts that are very good investments that pay yields in the 8% or even 12% range. Let's look to see what that does for our investment. Considering an 8% interest rate, we would end up with $321k. A 12% interest rate would give us $529k.

These examples show us that the yield of a dividend can be an important factor. But as we discussed in the first chapter, there are many factors to consider. So, let's say that we have a diversified portfolio of dividend investments and that the average interest rate is 5%. In that case, our 20-year investment plan nets us $225k. With a yield of 5%, if we start taking out dividends at that point, we can expect an annual income of about $11,250.

But suppose we increased our monthly contribution. This is difficult for a lot of people to do, but it shows the power of sacrifice in building wealth. Increasing our monthly contribution to $1,000 a month would turn the $225k earned earlier into $423k. That would also increase our annual income from the dividends to around $21,000 a year.

Time, of course, is the friend of the dividend investor. If we contribute $1,000 a month over 30 years, then we are going to end up with $840k.

Many readers are here because they don't have time. Maybe you've been going through life without a serious retirement plan, relying on a 401k or financial advisors. Or maybe you haven't invested at all. If you are older and seeking to build retirement wealth, the situation, sad to say, is far more difficult. That doesn't mean it can't be done, however, but it's going to take a lot more dedication and sacrifice.

Young people who are hoping to gain financial independence earlier are also going to be interested in this situation – so basically what we are talking about is trying to figure out a plan to generate wealth and income over a short time frame like 15 or even 10 years.

Let's look at the impact of making higher monthly contributions. If you can invest $2,000 a month, in ten years, you can generate a nest egg of $318,000. That is starting with the same $10k investment. Starting with a higher amount in your initial investment doesn't have as much impact. If you start out with $20k, you'll get to $334k, which isn't much higher.

Stock Appreciation

These examples are illustrative, but they fail to capture the true power of dividend investing. The reason is that in addition to interest, the value of your shares is going to be appreciating as well – assuming that you make wise choices in your stock picks.

Today, IBM is trading for around $140 a share, but back in the late 1990s, it was only trading for $45-

60 a share. Stock appreciation is a phenomenon that a regular savings account doesn't have. Of course, since you are picking dividend stocks, they are not going to grow at the same aggressive rate that the top growth stocks are going to be appreciated, but even so, you can see substantial appreciation over ten and twenty-year periods. Assuming that the yield remains constant, or even grows, you can get even better results than those we've described so far. According to dividend.com, dividend-paying stocks have averaged a total return of 11% over the past 75 years. Using that kind of return, it is more than possible to generate a half a million dollars in ten years, investing $2,000 a month. You will also be at a point where you can generate a sizable income. If you start earlier, of course, you will be in shape to earn a lot more. But the point is, even if you only have ten years to work with, if you are serious and committed, you can build up a nice retirement income.

So, don't give up, no matter your situation! It may take a lot of sacrifice in the near-term, but it can be done.

In fact, using the average 11% return, it's possible to invest $2,000 a month starting with $10,000 in your initial investment and end up with nearly a million dollars – in just 15 years.

DRIPS And Reinvesting For Long-Term Success

Many people give in to the temptation of cash in their hands, and it can be tempting to take the cash you get from dividend payments now. But if you have other sources of income and don't have a true emergency that dividend payments could solve – don't do it. Reinvesting the dividend payments is a vital component that you need to include in your wealth-building investment plan. It is only through reinvesting the dividends that you can get the kinds of scenarios that we have outlined here so far.

Many brokerages and companies offer DRIPS, which are dividend reinvestment plans. A DRIP is something you can set up to automatically reinvest your dividend payments. You can allow the DRIPS to remain in force until you reach retirement, ensuring that the dividend payments are used to buy even more shares of stock, continually growing your investment base so that it is as large as possible when you near retirement – whenever retirement is defined in your case. DRIPS even allow you to purchase fractions of a share, so that not a penny of your dividend payments is wasted. Smart investors always use DRIPS. You shouldn't start taking cash dividend payments until you have reached a point where you have a portfolio that is the size you need to earn a comfortable income.

Cash Flow And How Much Do You Need?

Professional investment advisors like Bob Brinker tell investors that they can take out 4% per year from their stock investments. In other words, we are talking about cashing out 4% of your investments in order to get the cash to spend. So, we are talking about not having dividend income. The idea of the 4% rule is that this is the maximum you can take out without running out of your investments. Hopefully, they will continue to appreciate at 4% or more, or over time the investments are going to be used up.

If you had $250,000 in stocks, this means that you could take out $10,000 per year. That's a nice shot in the arm, but it's not something that you can live on. If you are looking to achieve a middle-class lifestyle from the income generated by your investments alone, then we can use this example to estimate that we need at least $1,250,000 in order to pull it off.

That is not a trivial amount of money. Of course, if your investments are yielding higher rates, you won't need as much. In the end, sitting down and going through the numbers and planning out your future is one of the most important things to do. You don't want to suddenly find yourself at age 65 and discover that you are only able to generate an annual income of $8,000 or $12,000 from your investments. Think carefully now about how much you need to invest to generate a middle-class income, and also look at what you are investing in. Do you want to invest in Apple because you love your iPad? Probably a bad move. Yes, investing in Apple can be a good decision, but you need to consider how investing in Apple is going to generate income for you later. If income is what you seek, then investing in an IBM that pays more than twice the yield is a better choice.

Growth stocks can be a part of your overall strategy, even if you are hoping to live off dividend income in retirement. With growth stocks, you can get much higher levels of stock appreciation in some cases, and when you get closer to retirement, you can sell your growth stocks and then move that money into solid, dividend-paying investments.

Chapter 3: Manage Your Portfolio Using Fundamental Analysis

If you are going to become a self-directed investor, understanding fundamental analysis is going to be important. This may sound intimidating to many readers, but the reality is that fundamental analysis is based more on common sense than it is on financial expertise. You don't have to become a financial whiz to do fundamental analysis. You only need to learn what sorts of things you should look for in order to estimate the health of a company. Also, keep in mind that some mistakes are going to be made, and things can change. That is why we will emphasize diversification as a part of your overall investment strategy.

The Big Picture

So, what are we looking for in fundamental analysis? We are looking for characteristics and data that will support the notion that a company is a good investment. Some of the things that you'll look for are:

- Increasing revenue and profits.
- Consistent revenue and profits.
- A good management team.
- A company that manages debt well.
- Companies that invest in R & D, which generally means more long-term success.
- Upcoming products and services that hold promise and value – they don't have to be game-changers.

Basic Financial Statements

The first place you want to check when investigating the financial health of the company is to go over their recent financial statements. There are three statements that can be used to get a lot of information about the company, and publicly traded companies are required to provide audited statements to the SEC and general public, so this information can be generally considered as highly reliable. The financial statements that you want to look at are the income statement, the balance sheets, and cash flow.

Income Statements

An income statement is basically what the name implies. It's a statement showing the revenue the company earned over the period described by the income statement, along with expenses, gains, losses, and net income. On many publicly available income statements, you will see the past four years of data plus TTM, which means the trailing twelve months. You can get older data if you like, and this information can also be viewed on a quarterly basis. When viewing data on a quarterly basis, you should take care to make sure that you are comparing apples to apples so that you can avoid getting misled by seasonal variations, so compare each quarter of data to the like quarter in the previous year and so on.

The first items that you will want to draw your attention to in the report are total revenue and gross profit. You want to see revenue and profit increases over time, but there may be good reasons for explaining short-term decreases in profit. Sometimes a company may forgo profit if they are investing more revenue into building up inventories or doing research and development for example.

So, it's important to look at revenue, so you can determine whether or not the causes of any decline are external or internal. As we mentioned earlier, Amazon went for many years without making any profits at all. As a dividend investor, you are not going to be looking for aggressively growing companies, but if a company has missed a few quarters or even years of profit growth because they have been reinvesting money into company operations to lay the groundwork for future growth, this is generally acceptable.

A company might still be worth investing in over the long term if it has a solid history but had a few bad years or quarters. But if this appears to be the case, you'll want to check how the company is managing to pay dividends while it's fighting through bad times. If the company is stagnating or showed some revenue declines and it's a company with a long, solid history, if they kept up their dividend payments through the hard times, then this is a good sign that the company may still be a good investment.

The main things to look at are revenue and net income. You want to see solid annual growth rates of at least 5% per year, and if you don't see those growth rates, if there is not a good reason why they aren't there, then you should look elsewhere for your investments. You may also see a case where net income dropped for a company but then turned around. While the turnaround is a good sign, you'll want to do some research in order to determine what happened that led to these circumstances in the first place.

At the bottom of an income statement, you are going to see an item marked EBITDA. This means earnings before interest, tax, depreciation, and amortization. This is a net income plus interest, taxes, depreciation, and amortization. The purpose of this quantity is to eliminate some impacts of capital expenditures that can distort comparisons between one company and another, or between different sectors of the economy. This can help you determine what investments are the best ones for your particular situation.

Chapter 4: 7 Unbeatable Long-Term Investment Strategies

In this chapter, we are going to discuss strategies that are useful for long-term investment success. These strategies are well-known and have been proven time and again to be effective. The purpose of these strategies is to lower the inevitable risk that comes with any investment activity.

The fact is that no matter how careful you are or how thoroughly you investigate a company's fundamental characteristics and financial prospects, we can never tell the future. Some of the best companies are going to end up going out of business or bankrupt. Some of the companies that appear to be in trouble now are going to end up being the stars of tomorrow. Unless you have psychic abilities, it is basically impossible to know with any certainty which company is which. But we do know that if we pay careful attention to fundamental analysis on average, it is going to predict which companies proved to be successful investments. So, the key to a long-term investment strategy is to utilize this average behavior to your benefit. Generally speaking, that means investing in a large number of companies.

Before we get started, let's give an overview of the strategies that are used in a long-term investment portfolio. The first strategy is called diversification. The basic point behind this strategy is to avoid putting all your eggs in one basket. Next, we are going to consider a technique called dollar-cost averaging. These are the two main strategies that, combined with fundamental analysis and understanding of your overall goals, can lead to long-term success and wealth building.

Diversification

Everyone understands the basic idea behind diversification. It is this — none of us can predict the future with any certainty, and so it is impossible to know if any single individual company is going to prove to be a long-term success. Remember one of the most basic rules. Given enough time, anything can happen. Companies that seem invincible today might be bankrupt in 30 years. Building wealth and income using dividend investing means that you are going to be looking at longer time horizons. At the very least, you will be investing for a decade. History is littered with companies that either went out of business or had to undergo major restructuring in order to survive over the long term.

Just in recent memory, we have seen old financial stalwarts like Merryl Lynch, Lehman Brothers, and Bear Stearns Face bankruptcy and liquidation. Even General Motors, which at one time was one of America's greatest companies, had to run to the government to save itself from going out of business. If you had asked anyone in the 1960s whether any one of these companies would ever end up bankrupt or out of business, people would've thought that you were crazy.

So, although companies like Facebook, Apple, and Amazon seem invincible right now, it is impossible for any of us to know what the long-term future is for these corporations. Given this fundamental fact, and approach toward investing was developed so that rather than staking your future on one company, you would reduce your risk by investing in multiple companies simultaneously.

If you have invested in 20 different companies, if one or two or even three of these companies end up in bankruptcy, your overall investment portfolio is going to remain in decent shape, maybe even great shape. This is the main principle behind this strategy. We are basically playing the odds that most companies that are carefully selected based on sound financial principles are going to hold up over the lifetime of our investments.

Secondly, diversification is going to help you build a stock portfolio that is likely to lead to higher returns. If you take a basket of companies, some are going to grow faster than average, some will be average, and others are going to fall behind and grow at the low average rates. Just like we can't predict which, if any companies are going to go bankrupt, we can't know for sure which companies are going to grow rapidly over the next 20 or 30 years, and which companies are going to stagnate or even grow at a slower than average rate. Since you can't know this ahead of time and the best metric for success is probably going to be selecting large numbers of companies to use in your portfolio.

Another factor that needs to be considered is the sector of investment. Besides dealing with individual companies, entire industrial sectors are going to face different futures. Of course, it seems inevitable that technology has a bright future. That is probably the case, but looking at all the sectors in the economy, it's not certain that anyone of them is going to be growing at the same rate in the future as it has been so far in the past. Remember that things are always changing in a dynamic economy.

Therefore, a diversification strategy in your investments has two legs. The first leg is that you should invest in at least 15 to 20 different companies. The second leg to the diversification strategy is that you should invest in multiple sectors of the economy.

So, it would be a mistake to have 20 investments in the high-tech sector. We can all probably agree that high-tech is not going anywhere, but that does not mean that the growth it has experienced over the past 20 to 30 years is going to continue indefinitely. For example, we all need utilities and electricity. But most of us recognize that as far as growth, those types of companies are not ideal by any means. But remember, at one time they were.

This means that in addition to investing in multiple companies, you should plan on investing in multiple sectors of the economy. This is one reason that the unconventional investments that we discuss in chapter 7 are important. You can use those types of investments not only to increase your yields but also as a mechanism to increase the diversity of your investments.

Most readers are going to recognize the danger that an investor would face putting all of their investments into real estate. But the same readers might also be blind to the danger of investing in nothing but high-tech companies. If you are one of those people, it is important to recognize that diversity is important to apply in all cases. We simply cannot see the future, and investment always carries high risk. Therefore, it makes perfect sense to invest in multiple companies and sectors.

So, the question is, how much diversity is necessary in order to have a truly diversified portfolio?

One of the best answers to this question would be that you should be investing in hundreds, if not thousands, of companies. But this ideal answer has to be balanced against the realities of the human mind and how much one person who is not a full-time financial advisor can invest in truly analyzing the financial health and potential of multiple companies. There is an obvious point at which one person goes beyond their capacity to accurately make good investments.

The general rule that most financial advisors stood by is a good diversification level is about 15 to 20 companies.

In addition to this, we should add that a good investor should be investing in at least four different sectors of the economy. Within these rules, you can use your own criteria and interests to pick investments that you want to use. Of course, given the topic of this book, we hope that the reader would be using the criteria of good dividend investments when making their selections.

Index And Fund Investing

In Chapter 6, we are going to talk about index funds. One way that you can increase the diversity of your investments is by using index funds either for your entire portfolio or as a way to diversify your portfolio. There are many index funds to choose from these days, and they allow investors to spread their money around entire sectors or indexes in the economy.

As we will see, you can pick funds that allow you to invest in specific sectors of the economy or in large indexes such as the S&P 500. You can use funds to invest in healthcare, real estate, and other important areas and gain diversified exposure to hundreds if not thousands of companies and investments.

If you choose to go this route, the next question that follows is how many and what proportion to use? In other words, it's possible to build your own portfolio with some specific investments while adding fund investments to help increase diversity. There are no exact or right or wrong answers for this. What I would suggest for most people is that they should break it down 50-50. So, in this case, you might pick up 10 of your favorite companies that you want to invest in, and then pick a few phones to use for the rest of your investments. That way, you will have enough diversity in your portfolio to protect you from overall risk or the risk of being too heavily invested in a single company.

Something fundamental to keep in mind is that you should try to equally distribute your investment money so that you don't have diversity on paper while having most of your money tied up in one or two companies.

Dollar-Cost Averaging

Dollar-cost averaging is another technique used by experienced investors to reduce their overall risk. In this case, we are really engaging in diversity or diversification as well. Maybe you wouldn't think of it that way but that is really what it boils down to. Let's explain how that works.

What dollar-cost averaging means is that you invest your money in equal amounts and over equal time intervals. The purpose of doing this is to avoid the mistake of buying assets when they are actually at high prices. What do you want to do is spread around your investments so that your investments average out over time. This is a way to make sure that you get the best prices possible on average. Just like we can't predict if an individual company is going to go bankrupt in 10 years, it is difficult to say whether or not you are buying at a high or a relatively low at any given time. Since that is not something we can know with any certainty, although traders claim to be able to divine this information, dollar cost averaging gives us diversification with respect to the bullishness or bearishness of the market. The truth is if you use dollar-cost averaging at some points, you are going to be overpaying for your stocks. However, at other times, you are going to be buying stocks at a discount. So, as we stated already, these two extremes are going to average out over time.

Dollar-cost averaging is actually a simple process to implement. All you have to do to implement dollar-cost averaging is to decide on a regular investment schedule. So, you might invest in the 15th and the 30th of every month, for example. Then you put in equal amounts of money each time that you invest.

Rebalancing

Another important strategy used by long-term and income investors is called rebalancing. At the end of each year, you can examine your investment portfolio to see if it is still meeting your long-term investment goals. Securities that have grown outsized can be trimmed down by selling them off and reinvesting the money in areas that have declined. To use a simple example, suppose that you had determined that your investment goals would be met by having a portfolio consisting of 55% growth stocks and 45% in bonds. If at the end of the year the portion of your capital in growth stocks was 60% and now 40% in bonds, the rebalancing process would involve selling off enough stocks and then buying more bonds to restore the 55%-45% balance.

Rebalancing can also be used to keep your stock portfolio in the proportions that best meet your goals. So in other words, if you had Google, GE, and Boeing stock in proportions of 40-30-30, at the end of the year they might be 50-25-25, so you would want to sell some Google stock to rebalance the portfolio to 40-30-30 by buying up more stock in GE and Boeing.

When you are a dividend investor, you can also use rebalancing as a time to evaluate dividend performance. If you find that there are stocks with better yields or other properties that you feel would better meet your goals than the stocks currently in your portfolio, you can move money out of existing stocks and into the new stocks. You can also use your end of the year evaluation to do analysis on dividend payments and earnings and look for red flags such as a company that has not increased or kept up their dividend payments.

Fundamental Analysis Review

Once a year, after all, four quarters of the previous year's data are in, you can also stay on top of things by reviewing the financial statements of each company in order to check their financial health. Although we begin our investment lives excited about certain companies, there is no reason to stick with them to the end of their performance is not going to help us meet our investment goals.

Therefore, you should be constantly reviewing each of your investments and be ready to make changes if a company is showing signs that it is not going to be a good investment for you over the long-term. That doesn't mean you dump a company because they had one bad quarter or even a bad year. You will have to carefully evaluate each situation, in particular looking at what the company is doing to respond to declining market share or revenues, or if they have taken on a lot of debt what they are doing about it going forward. Obviously, life has ups and downs, and some companies are going to have some bad years, but they will still be solid long-term investments that you can count on for income down the road. But there are also going to be times when it is best to go ahead and sell off your investments in one company and look for greener pastures.

The Best Investment Strategy: Be Active

Don't be a blind investor. Most people go about their investment lives letting someone else manage it. They get a 401k through their employment or hire a financial advisor, and then they just let things sail along. The best advice for a self-managed investor is no matter what strategy you choose to pursue, stay on top of your investments. Keep up with financial and economic news, in particular as it relates to the companies that you have chosen to invest in. Keep on top of the company's financial statements, market performance, management team, and product development and releases. And be an active investor, who is not afraid to make changes when necessary.

Second, never stop your financial education. Keep up with the latest books, videos, and other information. Subscribe to leading financial publications so that you can stay on top of economic news. Listening to investment programs where advice is given, such as Ric Edelman or Bob Brinker, can be helpful as well. Brinker is no longer on the air, but you can get a lot of wisdom by subscribing to his newsletter and listening to his archives.

Avoid Panic

Finally, avoid panic. Novice investors always panic and sell off all their shares and move into cash at the first sign of trouble. The thing to realize about recessions and panics is that they pass with time, and when you look back at the long-term history of the stock market, you will find that stock market declines are short-lived. Once you have started building up a stock portfolio for the purposes of dividend income down the road – you should stick to it through thick and thin and not vacate the market for cash, hoping to jump back in later. That kind of amateurish panic behavior is going to put you in a situation where you are going to be paying way too much for stocks, and you're basically starting all over again. Instead of taking that approach, you should use downturns as an opportunity to get cheap/discounted stocks.

Another strategy to employ is to put a certain percentage of your investments into funds that short the market. There are a few exchange-traded funds that do this. I would not advise putting a large percentage of your portfolio into them, but 3-5% would be reasonable. These funds gain a lot of value when there is a recession. So, you can buy into them when times are good, and then sell them when a recession hits for a major profit. Shares in these funds have been known to go up by as much as 720% or more in value when a recession hits. You can then use the profits to buy more dividend-paying stocks when they are selling at a discounted value, because of the recessionary conditions.

Chapter 5: The Key To Profitable Investing

Many readers have not done self-managed investing. Most of us get a job and have a company managing a 401k for us, or we hire financial advisors. Those who are bolder may invest in mutual funds, but that is still passive investing which is quite a bit different from picking individual stocks and making your own plans to build a dividend-paying portfolio.

With that in mind, in this chapter, we are going to cover the basics of self-directed investing. This will include a discussion of stockbrokers, what they do and how to go about selecting a brokerage. We will also discuss how to go about trading your own stocks and how to do important tasks like getting money in and out of your investments.

What Is A Brokerage

When people think of the stock market, they will usually think of the madness and chaos of the trading floor. You might have visions of a bunch of screaming people waving papers around and billboards with passing numerical data flashing on them.

It is true that the world exists to some extent, but when you become a self-directed investor, you're shielded from it. Investors don't place direct orders for stocks or other financial assets; rather, they go through a stockbroker. A stockbroker is nothing more than a middleman.

Let's take a step backward for a minute. What is a stock exchange? A stock exchange is just a place where there is a trading market. Traders – and stockbrokers buy and sell shares of stock at the stock exchange. As soon as stocks in public companies were created in the 17th and 18th centuries, markets arose where people would meet to trade their shares. So, it's not really anything more complicated than a flea market, but instead of trading used goods, people are selling shares of stock that they want to get rid of. Buyers bid up the price of those shares, or when there is no demand for them, people have to lower their prices until they are able to sell them off at the lower perceived value.

As soon as people began trading shares of stock, it became more official and actual "stock markets" were created. This type of business soon moved over to the new world where it took root in the area that would later become New York City. While there had been earlier stock exchanges, the first official stock exchange in the modern sense was set up in Amsterdam in 1611. It's no surprise that Wall Street, and its future role as a financial center, began in New York City since the area began its life as a Dutch settlement. The New York Stock Exchange was officially established by a small group of stockbrokers in 1792.

A brokerage is a company that plays a role as a stockbroker. They operate at the stock exchange for clients. Their main role is to buy and sell shares of stock on your behalf. They also maintain an account for you that can be used to collect money from selling stock or to fund the purchase of stock. They also keep records of your holdings and operate according to the laws and regulations of the Securities and Exchange Commission or SEC.

The stock market and stock brokerages have evolved rapidly with every technological advance. As soon as the telephone got widespread use, investors could call in orders via phone to their brokers. Pencil and paper gave way to computer technology, and by the mid-1990s stock brokerages began operating largely online. This development caused individual investment to grow by leaps and bounds. Being able to maintain accounts online, investors had access to real-time information about the markets and were able to place trades much faster than they had been able to do in the past. During this time period, newer brokerages like TD Ameritrade and E*TRADE rose to prominence.

The trend of technological development and ease of use has continued. Since the introduction of mobile apps, many brokerages have moved to provide mobile access that allows users to trade stocks with apps. New brokerages have opened such as Robinhood that are based almost entirely on mobile and allow commission-free trading.

Commissions are fees that stockbrokers used to rely on in order to make profits. However, in recent years the movement toward zero commission trading has accelerated. Brokerages are finding new ways to make money, by offering preferred or upgraded accounts, for example, and competition is forcing many of them to lower or eliminate commissions on individual trades.

This is great news for stock traders and individual investors. It's now far less expensive to trade frequently – in fact, on many brokers, it costs nothing at all. This means that you can easily take dollar-cost averaging to an extreme and buy stocks every day if you have the time and inclination to do so and can spread out your purchases that way. The fact is it's never been easier to trade stocks and manage an investment portfolio as an individual investor.

What A Brokerage Provides

The first thing that a broker provides is an account that can be used for trading, and to take out funds. This is a cash account. You will need to electronically connect a bank account to the account that is managed by your broker. Then the money can be transferred to and from the brokerage account.

When you are paid dividends, they will go into this account. The money can be taken out as cash, or you can reinvest the money to purchase more shares of stock. As we discussed earlier, you should be reinvesting all of your proceeds during the investment phase of your financial life so that over time, you can grow your account as large as possible.

Brokerages also provide an interface or trading platform that can be used to buy and sell stock and possibly other financial securities like options. To varying degrees, you will also be able to pull up information about any publicly traded company. Some brokerages offer extensive information, and if desired you may also be able to access the services of a professional financial advisor. If this is something that you feel you would like to use, then you are probably going to be more interested in a traditional brokerage like Charles Schwab or Fidelity.

Other brokerages are geared more to self-service, but they still provide extensive web-based tools that can be used to do fundamental and technical analysis of stocks and companies. They may include charting tools and other things you can use in order to do research into deciding when to enter your stock trades. Keep in mind that long-term investors are not really concerned with trading at the exact right moment; in fact, if you are using dollar-cost averaging, it shouldn't matter at all. One tool you will want to use if it's available is going over the dividend payment history of companies you invest in, which is often displayed on stock market charts.

The main part of a trading platform is the ability to place your trades. Remember that a broker is a middleman and so you will electronically enter your trades with the broker, who actually carries them out for you. In today's world, since everything is electronic for all intents and purposes, trades occur in real-time.

Opening A Brokerage Account

Opening a brokerage account is pretty simple. The first step is to get online and do some research to find an US or home-based brokerage firm that you like. Visit their websites and, if possible, read reviews by stock market experts and individual investors. You can do comparison shopping based on features, but most brokerages offer pretty much the same features these days. As we mentioned earlier, one differentiating factor may be the ability to get assistance from a professional financial advisor, and some sites are going to have more in-depth research tools than others. Which features are going to be important are going to be up to you; this kind of decision is pretty much a personal one.

Once you choose a broker, you can apply to open an account. Different levels of information may be required by different brokers, but it will be pretty standard for the most part. Some may require government-issued ID or proof of residence, and you will have to connect a checking account and fund your account with the broker to get started.

Placing Your First Trades

Once you have successfully opened and funded your brokerage account, it's time to start building up your portfolio! But before you actually start placing trades, it's a good idea to get a notebook and write out a trading plan. Your trading plan is not something that is going to be set in stone; obviously, you can adjust it as conditions warrant. But the trading plan should include some of the following information:

- Frequency of investing: Adopt a dollar-cost averaging strategy. Ideally, the more often you invest the better, but pick an investment frequency that works for your situation.

- Amount to invest: the best way to build up a dividend-paying portfolio of stocks is to specify an amount to invest in regular intervals. Be realistic, and don't pick an amount that you are going to have trouble investing. The key is to make sure you invest something at regular intervals. If you pick a figure that is too high, you might find yourself missing investment targets and, in many cases, not investing at all. Remember that you can always invest more, and you can adjust your investment targets when you have more ability to devote funds to this purpose.

- Specify your portfolio. This step is going to take research, and therefore time. But you should pick out the companies or funds that you want to invest in. Then you should weight them. How you do this is up to you.

- Keep a record. Record the trades you make in your trading plan as you make them, and also keep track of your overall portfolio.

Once a quarter, tally everything up and see if you are meeting your overall goals or not. Then make adjustments as necessary.

Once you have your trading plan in place and you have the funds in your brokerage account to begin trading, it is simply a matter of placing your first trades. Actually, trading is a very easy process. You will just look up a stock you are interested in, and then follow the onscreen prompts to place your buy orders.

Types Of Orders

To review, there are different types of orders that can be placed. You can place a market order, which is probably going to execute pretty quickly if the price of the stock is not moving dramatically fast. A market order simply places an order at the prevailing market price. You can also place a limit order, which means that you will only buy or sell stock at a price that you specify. A limit order may or may not execute; you have to find someone to take the other side of the trade at the price that you specify. Of course, if prices on the market move to the price that you put in your limit order, then the trades will execute. Limit orders can be placed to automatically cancel at the end of the trading day, or they can be placed as good until canceled, which means if the order is not filled you have to cancel it manually.

When placing limit orders, be sure to look at the bid and the ask. A bid is the price buyers are currently offering. Ask is the price that sellers are currently asking for the stock.

Withdrawal Of Profits

If you sell a stock, or you get paid dividends, this will show up as cash in your brokerage account. Generally, there is a time delay of a few days before you can actually pull out this cash and move it to your bank account. The process is pretty straightforward, however; you just specify the amount you want to withdraw and then click a couple of buttons, and the money will be wired to your bank. Remember that you are going to be responsible for paying any taxes. And once again, we must emphasize that while you are growing your portfolio, you shouldn't take out dividend payments. Set up DRIPS to have them reinvested automatically if you are able to do so.

Having More Than One Brokerage Account

You can have more than one brokerage account. One of the easiest ways to get started is to use an account you may already have. As a part of your 401k plan, for example, you might already have an account at a firm like Fidelity. You can also use that to open an individual account and place your own trades. Another possibility is to open an individual retirement or IRA account. All of this can be done in conjunction with your original 401k.

It's also possible to open accounts at different brokerages. There really isn't a reason to do so, but some people may wish to avoid having everything riding on one brokerage. Others might want to try out different brokerages to find the one that they like the best.

Protection Against Loss

Bank accounts are insured by the federal government up to certain amounts. People wonder if their investments in stocks are insured, and what about the brokerage? Like any business, a brokerage can go bankrupt and be liquidated. What happens then? This is an important thing to be aware of, for obvious reasons.

Let's tackle investments first. Are you protected against losses in investments? That is if you buy a stock and it becomes worthless, do you get your money back, or a portion of it back? The answer is, no you do not. Investments in stocks are not protected in any way. When you buy a stock, you are knowingly assuming the risk that the stock might lose its value. So, you receive zero protection for this in the vast majority of cases. If there was some kind of fraud involved, then maybe you could get a portion or all of your money back. But if the loss occurs in the normal course of business, you are definitely not getting your money back.

What about cash? Cash in a brokerage account is a different story. This is managed by an analog to the FDIC, called the SDIC. The job of the SDIC is to cover cash losses in the event that your broker goes bankrupt, and the cash in your brokerage account is lost. Like a bank account, the SDIC will cover up to $250,000 in cash that is lost in a brokerage account. If you invested with ABC Brokerage, and they declare bankruptcy, and you had $350,000 in cash in your ABC account, the SDIC would pay you $250,000. So, you will be out any cash that goes above the $250,000 threshold. If your friend Betty had $175,000 cash in her ABC account, since it is below the threshold, she would get all of her cash back.

Now let's turn our attention to the issue of the stock itself. Your stock stays with you. If a brokerage goes out of business, typically there is an arrangement to move shares to another brokerage. You own the stock, not the brokerage, and so the stock is yours no matter what happens to the brokerage. You are at no risk of losing holdings of stock at any time no matter what happens to a specific broker.

As far as the cash is concerned, there is no reason to put more than $250k in cash in a brokerage account anyway. Any cash that you are seeing as profit should be moved to your bank account. Any cash that is not taken as profit should be invested. It's a good rule to never have a large amount of cash just sitting there in your brokerage account. You invest in stocks to make your money work for you; if it is not being put to any use, then you might as well stuff it in your mattress. Money that is not being used for investing should be moved to your bank account.

Margin Accounts

A margin account is one that allows you to borrow money from the stockbroker. By law, you are required to deposit $2,000 to open a margin account. After that, you can borrow money to buy stocks using 2:1 leverage. While margin accounts are useful for traders, using margin to buy stocks for the purposes of long-term investing and dividend investing is not something that should be pursued. Remember that although it would allow you to buy more stocks, you have to pay interest on any money borrowed from the broker. Traders use this approach because they will pay the broker back over a short time period. But there is no reason to borrow to buy stocks, which is a money-losing proposition in many cases. You wouldn't want to buy stocks using a credit card. This is only slightly better. Only use margin accounts if you are engaging in short term trading, which is not a subject covered in this book.

Chapter 6: Winning The Investment-Game Using Mutual Funds and Exchange Traded Funds

Diversification is one of the most important principles for successful long-term investing. That holds true when picking dividend stocks as well. One of the most frequently used tools to get diversification in a stock portfolio is to buy shares in mutual funds or the newer model of exchange-traded funds. You can also do this if you are building a portfolio of dividend-paying investments, but there are some upsides and downsides to taking this approach. In this chapter, we are going to introduce the concepts of mutual funds and exchange-traded funds and explain how they differ from each other. We will also take a look at using these types of investments to generate dividend payments. Finally, we will consider the advantages or disadvantages.

The Idea Behind A Fund

Earlier, we discussed the advantage of diversification. The more you can diversify your portfolio of stock holdings, the more resistant it is against being taken down by one or two or a small number of bad investments. Large and institutional investors are going to be able to invest in dozens, if not hundreds, of stocks. That gives them a major advantage, putting them in a position where they can track the market itself, rather than being beholden to a single company and its fortunes.

Doing that kind of investing simply isn't something that is available to an individual investor picking a few stocks. The more stocks you pick, the less money you're going to be able to put into any one investment, which means you'll be missing out on opportunities. Your investments would be spread so thin that it would be virtually meaningless because even though you'd be spreading your investments thinly, you wouldn't be able to have true levels of diversification.

But something even more important than this is the fact that when you start talking about investing in more than 15-20 companies, the level of information involved is simply too much for an individual to keep track of unless you are a full-time stock trader. The level of study that you want to use for fundamental analysis and determining what companies you want to invest in would require a level of time that most people simply don't have. You'd also have to devote full-time energy to tracking the companies you were investing in. If you have the ability to invest full-time and can support yourself, maybe you would be able to invest in 30 or 40 companies and be able to thoroughly analyze each one.

But that just isn't the reality that most people are facing. Most people have a full-time career or own a business and are investing on the side to build up some wealth for retirement. So, they have limited amounts of time that they can devote to picking stocks for investment and then tracking those investments once they've committed to them.

These ideas led may financial experts to start thinking of ways to give ordinary investors exposure to the kind of diversified portfolios that they would need to have true diversity. The way that it's done is by putting money from a large number of small investors into a pool, creating a fund. Then the fund would be used to buy dozens if not hundreds of stocks.

The fund itself could then be divided into shares. So, we could get all our friends together and collect a million dollars. Then we would buy a million dollars' worth of stock in companies on the S & P 500. The fund is now worth something by itself as a financial instrument since it owns stock in S & P 500 companies. At inception, it's worth a million dollars. So, we could slice up the million dollars into $10 shares and sell those shares in the fund itself. At $10 a share, we'd be able to issue 100,000 shares.

The shares themselves can then be traded, and their value would be derived from the underlying stock holdings. So, their value would fluctuate along with the stock prices of the companies in the S & P 500.

Mutual Funds

We've basically described the concept of a mutual fund. It's nothing more than a pooled fund of money collected from investors, which is then used to buy financial assets. There are mutual funds that buy all kinds of assets, from stock in the companies that make up the Dow Jones Industrial Average, to buying gold or buying treasury bonds. If you aren't familiar with mutual funds, there are some things to know about them before you jump on board and start buying up shares (or units as they are sometimes called) in mutual funds.

The first thing to know about a mutual fund is that they only trade once per day. They do not trade like stocks. At the end of each trading day, the mutual fund share value is reconciled with closing prices of the stocks that it holds to get a new value. The price of a share is called the Net Asset Value, or   NAV.

This is important to know because if you see a big movement on the stock market and place an order to buy or sell shares in a mutual fund that would be impacted by this price movement, you won't know the price that you'll get from the deal until the mutual fund is traded after market closing. This is a major downside of mutual funds that many people don't like. But for some investors, in particular, those who are long-term and hands-off investors that would rather let someone else handle their money, this won't be an issue.

That brings us to the next point, when looking into mutual funds you are going to want to know if the fund is managed or not. Of course, any fund has to be managed to some degree, if you are going to have a fund that tracks the S & P 500 or some other index, the company that sets up the fund is going to have to buy shares in the companies that make up the S & P 500. And as the members of the index change, the fund is going to have to buy and sell shares in order to reflect those changes.

However, some funds are professionally and actively managed. An actively managed fund will seek to beat the market. So, if you have an actively managed fund that tracks the S & P 500, it's not going to be blindly investing in the S & P 500 buying equal amounts of shares in all the companies on the index. Instead, the professional money manager is going to assign weightings to each of the stocks that make up the index. Then he or she will buy more, and fewer shares respectively, of stocks that they believe will be performing better or worse in the coming months. They will be constantly adjusting the holdings of the fund as they see fit, in order to maximize the performance of the fund. The idea is to give more weighting to better-performing stocks on the index so that the fund can actually provide better returns than the index itself provides.

Of course, if you have a professional money manager doing all that work for you, they aren't going to be doing that for free. This brings us to another issue associated with mutual funds, and that is costs and fees. Since mutual funds are run by a financial company, there can be many costs and fees associated with them. These are driven even higher when there is a professionally managed fund where stocks are constantly bought and sold as part of a strategy, but there are also basic expenses associated with any mutual fund. They have to pay for their fancy and slick brochures and a prospectus. They have to pay employees that run the office, and they have to pay to keep the lights on and so forth.

If a fund has a professional money manager that is handpicking investments, this is said to be an actively managed fund. You can cut costs by investing in a passively managed fund, but you might be giving up some performance.

Mutual funds charge commissions that are called "loads." A load is a sales commission that is charged when shares are bought or sold. A no-load fund does not charge sales commissions. Let's say for the sake of example that a fund that charges a commission has a $500 charge for a $10,000 investment in the fund. What this means from a practical standpoint is that if you invest $10,000 in the fund, you're going to be paying them a $500 commission, and only $9,500 is actually going to be invested.

In contrast, if you invested with a no-load fund, this means that your entire $10,000 would be invested. So, whether or not a mutual fund charges a load is something very important to note. The more you invest in the fund, the greater the difference there is in what you are actually investing and what you could invest going somewhere else.

Load Or No-Load Mutual Fund

So, the purpose of the load is to pay the professional investment team to manage the fund. They claim that their funds outperform no-load funds, and maybe they do in some cases. But you have to ask yourself if they outperform no-load funds to a high enough degree that they make paying the load worth it to the investor. Prior to investing, you should be very clear about the fees that a mutual fund company is going to charge and compare this to offerings from competitors so that you can find the right fit for your situation. You should include an analysis of the past performance of the funds, comparing them against each other, in order to determine whether or not investing in a fund with a load is worth it or not.

Another factor is thinking about how much of a do-it-yourself investor you really are. If you are not comfortable taking total control over your investments, then you can opt to go with mutual funds that are professionally managed and charge loads. However, if the idea of investing in mutual funds is an attractive idea, but you are more of a do-it-yourself type, you can invest in no-load mutual funds. One example of a large company that provides many no-load mutual funds is the highly regarded Vanguard, which manages several trillion dollars in investments.

Taking Diversity To Another Level

Mutual funds do more than let you invest in various stock market indices. They also allow you to get diversified exposure to a wide array of financial securities. For example, you can do sector investing, and gain exposure to entire sectors of the economy like energy, healthcare, or real estate. You can also use mutual funds to get exposure to foreign stock markets like Europe, Japan, or Canada. There are also many mutual funds that allow you to invest in emerging markets like China and Brazil. A big advantage when it comes to all of these investments, especially in foreign markets, is that it puts a layer between you and your actual investment. For example, when investing in foreign markets, if you did it directly, you would have to move your capital into the countries that you wanted to invest in, and then you would be subject to their laws. Your investments would lack the kinds of protections that are provided inside the United States by the FDIC, SDIC, and SEC. Furthermore, there may be more bureaucratic hurdles to cross and getting your money earned from overseas stocks into the United States might be difficult, and you might even have to worry about foreign exchange for currency.

The advantage of using a mutual fund is the fund will be dealing with all that, and as far as you're concerned, you're just doing another domestic investment.

Mutual funds also help you diversify your investments by enabling you to invest in corporate bonds, junk bonds, and government-issued bonds of all types. So, with mutual funds, it is possible to build up a completely diversified income-generating portfolio that uses many different stocks, sectors of the economy, financial instruments, and even countries or regions where your money is invested.

Pros And Cons Of Mutual Fund Investing

Mutual funds have many pros and cons. Let's summarize the pros:

- Diversified exposure.
- Easy, and good for hands-off investors.

- It can invest in a wide array of financial instruments.

The cons are:

- Often have high fees, commissions, and expenses.
- Only trade once per day.

Now let's have a look at the first cousin of mutual funds, the exchange-traded fund.

What Is An Exchange Traded Fund?

So, we see that mutual funds have some advantages and some disadvantages. The main advantage of mutual funds is that it simplifies investing and provides small investors with a way to get massive diversification. If you invest in mutual funds, you will be able to invest in any stock market index, any sector, and get exposure to other types of investments such as corporate bonds, treasuries, and overseas investments, including in emerging markets.

As we have seen, two disadvantages of mutual funds are that they have high levels of expenses (the more professional management, the higher the level of expense) and they only trade after market close.

The idea of an exchange-traded fund or ETF is to take the good things about mutual funds and get rid of the bad things. An ETF is basically a no-load mutual fund that trades like a stock. So, with an exchange-traded fund, you get the best of both worlds.

Buying shares of an exchange-traded fund is quite easy and accessible. You buy shares in them just like you would any stock like Apple, Ford, IBM, or Facebook. You just have to know the tickers. There are fees associated with exchange-traded funds, but the funds are minimally managed and so the fees are quite small. Since they trade like stocks, you can buy and sell shares in exchange-traded funds at any time the markets are open. There are also options for any exchange-traded fund on the market.

Many companies offer exchange-traded funds, but the leading companies include State Street SPDR, iShares, ProShares, and Vanguard. You can do research on the websites of these companies to find the highest performing funds. Many of them have amazing levels of returns that are 8-15% annually.

While mutual funds continue to thrive, exchange-traded funds have basically made them redundant. There would only be one reason to invest in mutual funds as opposed to just finding ETFs on the stock market. And that would be in the case where you really don't want to be a do-it-yourself investor and you would prefer the assistance and expertise of a professional money manager. If you want someone watching closely over your investments, then mutual funds are more your style. If you are interested in the diversification of mutual funds but would prefer taking direct control over your own investments, exchange-traded funds are probably more your style.

Like mutual funds, there are exchange-traded funds you can invest in that cover just about every financial asset under the sun. So, you can have a diversified portfolio that includes stocks, bonds, real estate, and commodities, but it would be entirely stock market based. There is a reason that exchange-traded funds have become very popular in recent years – they are an investor's dream.

Dividends And Fund Type Investing

Of course, this is a book about dividend investing, and so we need to look at how dividends are impacted when it comes to investing in these types of funds. You can collect dividends from both mutual funds and exchange-traded funds if the funds hold stocks that pay dividends. The way that the dividends are paid out is the fund collects all the dividends that are paid on the stocks in the holdings in the fund, and then these are divided up by the total number of shares in the fund. Then the dividends are either paid out or reinvested.

You will have to look at the specific rules for any fund that you invest in. Mutual funds may allow you to select a "growth" option for the fund, which would mean that any dividends paid out on your holdings are reinvested to buy more shares in the fund. In many exchange-traded funds, it is up to the fund manager as to whether or not dividends are distributed as cash payments or they are reinvested.

One of the implications of the way these funds are constructed is that you are going to receive relatively low dividend payments as compared to investing in any specific stocks. This is because typically, not all the stocks in a given fund will pay dividends. Since the dividend payments are added up and then divided by the number of shares in the fund in order to arrive at a per-share dividend payment, this value is going to be typically lower as compared to investing in something like IBM.

There are many exchange-traded funds that are geared toward dividend-paying stocks. However, you may find that here, too, the yields are relatively low as compared to many of the top dividend-paying stocks.

There is an interesting way that you can use exchange-traded funds to drive your investments, even if you are only looking to build a dividend income. If you are looking to reinvest your dividend payments anyway, one approach that can be taken with the long-term in mind is to invest in several exchange-traded funds that show appreciation rates that are higher than the market average. By choosing several high growth funds to invest in, you can grow your investment base at a rapid clip.

Then when you are nearing the point where you'd like to retire, you can move the money out of the exchange-traded funds and into specific dividend-paying stocks that have high yields, and that can generate the kind of annual income from stocks that you are looking for.

Just as an example, the exchange-traded fund QQQ tracks the top 100 companies on the NASDAQ. At the time of writing, the fund has an astounding year-to-date growth of 25%. The yield is only 0.8%, but you can ignore that and invest in QQQ for the sole purpose of growing your investment base, as opposed to IBM (say), which has much lower rates of growth but pays a 4.88% yield. So, the plan would be to invest in funds like QQQ until retirement, then when you are nearing retirement, you begin selling off shares in the exchange-traded funds and start buying shares in companies like IBM that pay high yields.

The reality is that exchange-traded funds provide you a lot more growth but yields that are not all that great. To get a $50,000 a year dividend income from exchange-traded funds is something that would require the purchase of a large number of shares.

Balancing A Portfolio

Another strategy that can be utilized that includes exchange-traded funds or mutual funds is as a fraction of a larger portfolio. In this strategy, you can pick 5-7 companies that you want to invest in, and then put 35-50% of your capital into funds rather than individual stocks. This can help you to diversify your overall portfolio while still retaining some direct control over investments in some of your favorite companies.

Top Picks For Dividend-Paying ETFs

If you decide to invest in dividend-paying exchange-traded funds, there are many to choose from. When researching funds to invest in, you'll want to look at several factors. The first, of course, is the yield. However, when investing in dividend-paying funds, it has to be said that, to a certain extent, you are making a tradeoff between the yield and the diversification that you get by investing in funds rather than individual stocks. Nonetheless, there is a lot of variety out there, and it's possible for anyone to find an acceptable yield. Second, you'll want to look at the expense ratios of the fund, although exchange-traded funds tend to have pretty low expenses as compared to mutual funds. So, in most cases, this is probably not going to be an issue to worry too much about.

Next, you'll want to look at the past growth history of the fund. Check the year to date returns, and also look at the historical growth. Most companies that offer exchange-traded funds make this information rather transparent so that it's easier for you to find a fund that meets your own investment goals.

When you are doing research on exchange-traded funds, you are going to find that they also list their investment objectives. This information is also provided with mutual funds, and it will help you pick the funds that are the most suitable for helping you to meet your investment goals. Personally, I like using exchange-traded funds for aggressive growth purposes, with the relative safety factor that comes with the diversification that they offer.

In this section, we will recommend some funds that you can start investing in. Some will have better dividend yields than others.

Vanguard High Dividend Yield Index Fund (VYM)

This is a very appealing fund. At the time of writing, it's trading at a modest price of $88.93 per share, making it a very appealing buy for investors that are looking to start building up their investments in dividend-paying stocks. It has also had a low expense ratio at only 0.06%, with a healthy year to date return of 17%. Even better, the yield is 3.16%. This is a very good yield, beating out many stocks that people like to invest in to receive dividend payments. This fund is very diverse – with holdings in 406 different stocks. Some of the funds top holdings include JP Morgan & Chase, Procter & Gamble, Johnson & Johnson, Verizon, Intel, and Chevron.

iShares Core High Dividend ETF(HDV)

Exchange-traded funds offered by iShares are run by the famed investing and financial management company Blackrock. These are very popular funds, although it's hard to top Vanguard when it comes to popularity. HDV is a high yield dividend fund, with a healthy yield of 3.33%. It hasn't performed as well as VYM lately, the year-to-date return checks in at 15%. Since the inception of the fund, it's provided an 11% annual return. With a share price of $93, it's in the same price range as VYM. HDV has holdings in 74 different companies. Some of the top holdings in the fund include A T & T, Wells Fargo, Pfizer, and Procter & Gamble.

SPDR SDY

SDY is the S & P dividend fund offered by State Street. The investment rating company Morning Start has rated this fund five stars. The yield is slightly lower, at 2.45% as compared to the first two funds that we looked at. The expense ratio is also quite a bit higher at 0.35%, but the year to date growth is a healthy 18%.

Invesco High Dividend Yield Financial ETF (KBWD)

This fund stands out for its high yield and low share price. The yield at the time of writing checks in at 8.76% and the share price is only around $21 a share. The fund is primarily invested in financial companies that are listed on the Nasdaq Financial Sector Dividend Yield Index. The holdings are of publicly traded financial companies, but they are probably not companies you are familiar with as household names. Despite the high dividend yield and narrow focus of the fund, it has a respectable year-to-date return of 14.86%. The high yield makes this fund a definite consideration to add to your investment portfolio, but the narrow focus on finance means that you probably don't want to make it too large a percentage of your overall investments.

Wisdom Tree Small Cap Dividend Fund (DES)

It can be helpful to diversify your investments among different sized companies, and this fund can help you load up on some small-cap stocks that are also paying dividends. This fund is also relatively inexpensive, trading at $27.67 a share. The yield is relatively modest at 2.84%, and although small-cap stocks are generally thought of as having high growth potential, the year to date return on this fund is 15.64%. While comparable to the other funds we've looked at, this is also a bit on the slower growth side. Nonetheless, a fund like this can help you diversify your overall portfolio at least during the growth phase of your investment life.

Chapter 7: How To Invest In Dividends And Save On Taxes Big Time

Many readers either have an individual retirement account or IRA, or you may be interested in setting one up as a part of your overall investment strategy. An IRA is a way to take advantage of tax breaks when setting up your retirement plan, and it is a good way to build up retirement funds for those who are not doing so through an employer. Even many readers who are using an employer-based plan will be interested in using an IRA to help them build up more funds for retirement.

What Is An IRA?

Just to make sure everyone understands what we are talking about, let's get started by defining what an IRA or individual retirement account is. An individual retirement account is an individually directed retirement account – no surprises there. The idea behind this type of account is that you are able to get some tax advantages by using an IRA as compared to just buying stocks. There are two options that are generally available in this regard. The first is that you get a tax break now on money used to deposit and invest in your IRA. The other option is to pay taxes now, and then you will be able to withdraw money from the IRA as tax-free income in the future.

Both approaches have merit. Given the current spending environment in Washington DC, it might be a good bet to have a retirement account where you can grow the money over time and then take it out tax-free when you retire. Unfortunately, the law restricts who is able to do what in that regard, as there are income limitations that we will discuss in a moment.

An IRA is not an investment in and of itself. Rather an IRA is an account that will hold investments. So, you will deposit money into an IRA, and then make investments in the IRA using that money. Money can be contributed once a year as a lump sum, or you can make periodic deposits to the account as long as you don't exceed the contribution limits.

There are many places where you can open an IRA, and you can open an IRA at a bank. However, if you are reading this book, you probably don't want to do that. Opening an IRA at a bank might be a way to save money, but you won't be able to invest in stocks – or in dividend-paying stocks – if you open an IRA at a bank. So, you should open an IRA at a stock brokerage. You can have a regular stock brokerage account and an IRA at the same broker, and both will be accessed through your same login.

Traditional IRA

A traditional IRA is one that is set up to take tax deductions now. So, any money that you deposit into a traditional IRA in the present time can be deducted from your taxable income.

Unfortunately, Congress places limitations on how much you can contribute to an IRA since this would cut into their tax revenue. As of 2019, you can contribute up to $6,000 to a traditional IRA account per year. If you are 50 or older, a "catch up" provision allows you to contribute $7,000 per year.

An IRA does not preclude you from using other savings and investment tools. You can have an IRA and also do self-managed investing in buying individual stocks. You can also have an IRA together with an employer managed 401K plan.

There may be some limitations on the ability to take the tax deductions on contributions to a traditional IRA. You will have to speak with a tax professional about this to address your own specific situation.

With a traditional IRA, you will be taxed on the gains when you withdraw funds from the account.

They love to tout the fact that your investments will grow tax-free while in the account, but under present law, this is true of any investment. Whether or not taking tax deductions now versus waiting until the future is beneficial is anyone's guess. As we noted earlier, given the prolific spending problems in Washington, they are probably going to be more tax hungry in the future than they are now. If you qualify for a Roth IRA (see below,) then that is something you should strongly consider, but if the government needs money very badly, the laws regarding Roth IRAs may change as well. You should also have some awareness that the possibility probably exists that at some point gains inside a growing individual retirement account could be taxed even without withdrawals. Although this hasn't been specifically discussed, there are already proposals in Congress to tax "unrealized" gains, which could mean taxing your growing funds inside of an individual retirement account.

There are no specific requirements to qualify for a traditional IRA. At this time, anyone can open an IRA and make contributions to it. One thing to be aware of is that while you are allowed to have an IRA and a retirement plan through an employer at the same time, this can impact the ability to deduct contributions to the IRA from your taxes. The amount that you can deduct can either be reduced or even be completely eliminated, depending on the level of your income. If you have a spouse that has an employer retirement plan, this can also impact your ability to deduct contributions to an individual retirement account. Income does not impact the ability to deduct contributions to a traditional individual retirement account if you don't have an employer directed retirement account.

Of course, laws are subject to change, but let's take a brief look at the tax deduction rules. If you are married and filing jointly and also have a retirement plan through an employer, you can take the full deduction for contributions to a traditional IRA provided that your adjusted gross income is $103,000 or less. If it is more than this amount but still less than $123,000, you are allowed a partial deduction. If your adjusted gross income is higher than this amount, you cannot deduct any contributions to an IRA.

If you are married and filing jointly, and you don't have a retirement plan through your employer but your spouse does, the income levels are raised to $193,000 or less for the full deduction, between $193,000 and $203,000 to take a partial deduction, and income above $203,000 you get no deduction. If you are married and filing separately, there is no full deduction allowed if you or your spouse has a retirement plan through an employer.

For those who are single or filing as head of household and have an employer-sponsored retirement plan, you can take the full deduction for IRA contributions provided that your adjusted gross income is $64,000 or less. If your income is higher than this but less than $74,000, you qualify for a partial deduction. If your income is above $74,000, you cannot take a deduction for IRA contributions.

If you don't have an employer-sponsored retirement plan, then you can deduct the full amount of your contributions from your income taxes.

As we will see in the next section, the amount of income you are earning has an impact on the type of IRA that you can open. A traditional IRA has no income limits.

The second thing to be aware of with the IRA is the age limit. If you withdraw any money before the age of 59 ½, you have to pay taxes on the money, and you also have to pay an early distribution fee. As of 2019, the early distribution fee is 10% of the amount of money taken out of the account. There are some exceptions to this rule; please consult a tax advisor for details.

You are also *required* to take distributions starting at age 70 ½. A traditional IRA has a required minimum distribution, so even if you don't want to take cash out at that age, the law requires you to take out the minimum. You are also no longer allowed to make contributions to a traditional IRA account once you reach the age of 70 ½. So, while there are some tax advantages, you can see that an IRA has a lot of restrictions that you are not going to have just bought shares of stock on your own. When you are simply doing individual investing, you are going to be able to take money out or put money in at any time, but of course, you are going to have to pay appropriate taxes on your capital gains.

The IRS also requires you to file tax forms when contributing to an IRA. Form 8606 is used to track after-tax contributions to an IRA so that you are not taxed again later on when you pull the money out. But of course, predicting what the environment is going to be like in 20 or 30 years is anyone's guess.

Nondeductible IRA

A nondeductible IRA is just a traditional IRA where you don't deduct the contributions. Investment returns in the account are not taxed until you withdraw them from the account. However, it gets a little convoluted. Since the deductions were never taken for contributions to the account, money that was originally contributed to the account won't be taxed with you withdraw it. Under the standard scenario where you deduct your contributions to the traditional IRA, assuming that you are able to do so, you will be taxed on the entire withdrawal when you take the money out. Under the scenario of the nondeductible IRA, you are only going to be taxed on your gains. As we will see, you can also convert a nondeductible IRA into a Roth IRA. We will discuss how that works in a minute, first, let's define what a Roth IRA is and go over the income limits associated with it.

Roth IRA

Like a traditional IRA, a Roth IRA offers you tax-free growth on the money that you invest in the account. But the big benefit of a Roth IRA is that when you pull the money out of the account during retirement, you can do so tax-free under current law. However, with a Roth IRA, you cannot deduct the contributions to the account from your current taxes.

So, with a traditional IRA, it deducts now and pays taxes later. With a Roth IRA, its pay taxes now, and get tax free income down the road in retirement. If the tax rate is expected to be higher in the future, then a Roth IRA makes good sense. Of course, whether it is higher or not in the future depends both on the political climate and economic situation, as well as on what your income happens to be in retirement. If your income in retirement is going to be relatively low, the tax benefits of a Roth IRA might not be that significant. On the other hand, if you have a high income in retirement, having the ability to take tax-free distributions from the Roth IRA can be a very nice benefit indeed.

Just like with a traditional IRA, you are limited as to the amount of money that you can contribute to a Roth IRA. As of 2019, you can contribute up to $6,000 if you are under the age of 50. Those who are 50 or older are able to contribute up to $7,000 per year.

When thinking about an IRA, it's important to think about the difference between the money you've contributed to the account and money that is earned from investments in the account. Since you have already paid taxes on money that has been deposited into an IRA, you can withdraw cash from the account up to the amount that you've contributed without restriction. That means that you can withdraw contributed funds from the account without paying any taxes or penalties. Of course, this would defeat the purpose of having the IRA – you put money in the IRA so that you buy stocks to grow your wealth over time. Second, you will be taxed on any investment earnings that you cash out of a Roth IRA if you take them out early.

Once again, the cutoff age for penalties is 59 ½. There is also a restriction that you must hold an IRA account for a minimum of five years. If both requirements are met, then you can take money out of the Roth IRA including any earnings and you will owe no federal tax on the money. You may owe state taxes. So, if you open a Roth IRA at age 58, you have to wait five years until age 63 before you can start taking the money including investment earnings out tax-free. Another benefit of the Roth IRA is that there is no minimum distribution requirement. Remember that if you open a traditional IRA, you are required to start taking minimum withdrawals at age 70 ½. In this case, you can wait if you want to, and a Roth IRA can even be passed on to your heirs.

Contributions to a Roth IRA are restricted to earned income. So, any money you get from capital gains or royalties cannot be contributed to a Roth IRA.

A Roth IRA sounds like a great deal, but there are strings attached. Eligibility for a Roth IRA is somewhat restricted. The first restriction is that you must have earned income. So basically, you have to have a job of some kind in order to contribute to a Roth IRA, or if you own a business, you have to be working as an employee of the business so that you are receiving regular, normal taxable income from employment.

Even worse, there are income limits for a Roth IRA. This is not about tax deductions; if your income is too high, you can't contribute to a Roth IRA at all. For a single filer, your adjusted gross income must be $122,000 or less in order to contribute to a Roth IRA using the full amounts. The amount allowed is reduced if you earn more than $122,000 but less than $137,000. If you are single and earn more than $137,000 a year (remember this is adjusted gross income), then you are not eligible to open a Roth IRA at all. If you have lower levels of earned income but get money from other sources such as capital gains, speak to a tax advisor to determine your eligibility to open a Roth IRA.

For married filing jointly, the cutoffs to contribute the maximum amount, partial amount, and not eligible at all are $193,000 or less, up to $202,999, and any income above $203,000 (again, these figures are for adjusted gross income). If you are married filing separately, you can only have

$10,000 a year in adjusted gross income to make partial contributions. Ponder the wisdom of Congress with that one.

The Backdoor Approach

Since a Roth IRA allows you to forgo taxes in the future when you withdraw the money, many people love the idea of a Roth IRA, but they might also find out they aren't eligible for one. This brings us back to the nondeductible IRA. It turns out that if you don't take any tax deductions with a traditional IRA, you can convert it into a Roth IRA without having to meet any income requirements.

The caveat here is that you must have paid taxes on any funds that have been contributed to the IRA. Unfortunately, if the account grows beyond your contributions, you'll also have to pay taxes on the gains if you do a conversion. But there is a backdoor way around this as well. You can make a lump-sum contribution to a traditional IRA account, pay taxes on the contribution, and then roll it over to a Roth IRA. You can actually repeat this procedure every year.

Dividend Payments And Growing Your IRA

Now let's get to the point of discussing individual retirement accounts in the context of dividends. One of the downsides of an IRA is that there are strict limitations on the annual contributions that you can make to your IRA. That is going to have implications down the road since you are going to be constrained in the overall growth of the account. Only being able to contribute $6,000 a year or $7,000 a year if you are 50 and over is a major restriction.

Wouldn't you like to be able to get around this restriction?

This is where dividends come in, and it's where we can tie everything together and build up an IRA to provide a nice account that is paying dividend income when you reach retirement. The key to this is the ability to grow your funds inside the IRA tax-free and without restriction.

By only investing in dividend stocks, you can ensure that you are getting dividend payments inside your IRA account. As your account grows, this is going to add up over time as you buy more stocks, and you're taking more dividend payments with each passing year. This will essentially allow you to get around the $7,000 contribution limit. By reinvesting any dividend income that you receive into your IRA, you are, in short, contributing more money toward growing the account.

When investing using an IRA for the purposes of making dividend payments, it should be used in conjunction with other means of investing. However, it can provide a useful tool to help you grow income over time. And if you are able to use a

Roth IRA, you may be able to realize substantial tax savings in the future. As we can all imagine, being able to take some tax-free income when we are in our retirement years would be a very large benefit.

The key here is that by taking dividends inside your individual retirement account, you will be able to get around the individual contribution limits without putting any extra cash into the account. In order to make this strategy work, you are going to want to find high yield investments. These can include exchange-traded funds, stocks, or some mixture of the two. But my preference would be for any investment that has a yield of about 5% or more. The higher the better, but be careful about any stocks you pick and do your due diligence (aka fundamental analysis) on any stocks that you invest in.

Chapter 8: 3 Unconventional Dividend Investments With "Unconventional" Gain-Potentials

To be honest, when it comes to dividends, this is one of my favorite topics. As a new investor, I think you are going to be excited about this too. In this chapter, we are going to go beyond conventional thinking about investing in stocks and consider investing in specialized companies that share their profits with investors. For all intents and purposes, these profit-sharing arrangements can be thought of as dividend payments, but in fact, in some cases, there are some really interesting tax advantages. You might call these types of investments as the secrets of the rich and famous. As you'll see, they allow you to take ownership stakes in a wide range of real estate, infrastructure, finance, and energy assets that until now you probably have not thought about investing in.

As with anything else, it's not a great idea to throw all of your eggs in one basket. So, you don't want to become so drawn in by the investments that we are going to be describing in this chapter that you don't invest in any conventional stocks. However, the investments in this chapter can and should make up a significant part of the portfolios of anyone who is building up an investment portfolio for the purposes of generating income.

How much should you put into these investments? My rule is about 15-45% of your investments can be put into these types of companies. Also, keep in mind that we are going to be describing quite a wide range of different types of investments and companies in this chapter. So, you are going to want to take a diverse approach here as well. Although we will be talking a great deal about different types of real estate, energy, and financial companies, the best plan is to spread the wealth around and invest in several of them, all across different sectors.

One advantage of some of the types of investments that we are going to describe in this chapter is they can help you weather economic downturns. While the fortunes of Amazon or Boeing might be tied directly to the overall economy, even when times are bad people are going to need nursing homes, energy, and other assets.

There are three basic types of companies that we are going to discuss in this chapter. They include real estate investment trusts, or REITs, Master Limited Partnerships or MLPS, and finally, we will discuss Business Development Corporations or BDCs.

One big advantage the companies discussed in this chapter have is that they are so-called pass-through entities. This means that they simply pass through profits to the investors, and they are not c-corporations. Publicly traded large corporations are c-corporations, and for investors, that is important because the earnings from c-corporations that are passed onto investors as dividends are subject to double taxation. That is, the corporation pays taxes on its profits and then pays out dividends, which are then taxed a second time. Of course, one time the corporation pays the tax, and the second time the investor pays the tax, but this taxing procedure ends up cutting into the potential profits that could have been paid out to investors.

In the case of pass-through entities, since they are not corporations, they are not subject to corporate taxes. Therefore, a higher level of revenues can be passed on to investors, and the earnings are only taxed once. Of course, as the investor, you have to pay the tax, but you are generally speaking paying tax on a higher level of income than you would be if these organizations were corporations and some of their profits were eaten up by corporate taxes.

So, there are three basic reasons to invest in these types of companies:

- You can diversify your stock investments even further, moving into real estate and energy investments.
- These are pass-through companies that can help you get a bigger slice of the earnings pie since no corporate taxes are involved.
- Many of these companies pay astoundingly high yields, which can help you get more return on your money, and when you retire you can collect a higher level of income for the same level of investment.

Let's get started by taking a look at Real Estate Investment Trusts. Then we will talk about Master Limited Partnerships, and then close out the chapter with a look at Business Development Corporations.

Real Estate Investment Trusts (REITS)

There are many ways that an investor can get involved with real estate. One way is to take on a lot of debt and buy lots of properties. Then you can rent them out and over the years, your renters will pay your mortgages off. Hopefully, you will make a little profit along the way, but the real hope will be that in retirement, your properties will provide you with a nice income stream.

Another way to get involved with real estate is through exchange-traded funds. You can invest in many different exchange-traded funds that are real estate oriented, allowing you to take advantage of the profits to be made in real estate, without dealing with the hassle of actual property ownership. Another advantage of using exchange-traded funds to invest in real estate overseas.

In this chapter, we are going to talk about investing in real estate directly, through entities that are called Real Estate Investment Trusts.

These are companies that own and generate profits from real estate. They are structured in such a way that they have to pass off most of their profits to investors.

While REITS are not corporations in the traditional sense, they are publicly traded on the stock exchanges. So, if one of the first questions that pop into your mind is how to invest in REITS – the answer is you do it through a stock brokerage account. And all you have to do is buy shares in REITS through your stockbroker in the same way that you would buy any shares of stock.

One of the beauties of REITS is that there are REITs for an incredibly wide range of properties. In fact, as we will see in a minute, there are REITs for properties that you wouldn't normally think of as real estate. But there are REITs for traditional real estate as well.

So, if you did nothing but invested in REITS, you could build up an incredibly diverse array of holdings. You can invest in REITs that operate single-family homes that are rented out, and you can invest in REITs that own office buildings. There is also a wide range of conventional real estate that is operated by REITS, including hotels and motels, shopping centers, hospitals, nursing homes, and warehouses. But there are also many assets that don't normally come to mind. For example, some REITs invest in ownership of cell phone towers. Other high-tech REITs invest in data centers that are used for cloud computing.

The applications of REITs seem almost endless. And while the economy has its ups and downs, as we said many of these facilities are going to be needed no matter what. That means that you can keep receiving a good income from the dividend payments that you get from REITs even during bad economic times. As with any investments, the key here is going to be diversity. If you put every last penny into single home rentals, then if this sector of the market runs into big trouble, then you are going to run into big trouble too. But if your investments in REITs are diversified, then you will be able to be earning money from some investments while others are not producing.

How Do REITs Work

REITs have been around for a long time. They were first created in the United States in 1960. The REIT structure has also spread beyond the United States into many different countries, facilitating global real estate investment. Whether you take advantage of that or not, there are certainly plenty of opportunities inside the United States.

A REIT has a general partner that manages the company. It can be a corporation, trust, or association. But the key fact about REITs is that they must pay out 90% of their profits to investors. This can mean that you will have the ability to invest in REITs that are often going to pay much higher yields than conventional stocks do. In the United States, it is estimated that REITs control $3 trillion worth of property. Even though REITs are required to pay out 90% of their taxable income to investors, in fact, many of them actually pay 100% of their taxable income to investors. Long-term capital appreciation helps REITs maintain solid dividend payments.

As an investor, you can invest in individual REITs that trade on the major stock exchanges, or you can invest in REITs through mutual funds or exchange-traded funds.

No matter how you decide to invest in REITs, if you choose to include some REITs in your overall investment portfolio, you are going to earn your money through the rents that the trust is collecting on its owned property. Just like a regular stock, over time, the share price of REITs can increase as well so that investors will benefit from capital appreciation as well as from the dividend payments that they receive. Moreover, you can take the same approach to REITs that you would with any other dividend producing investment. That is, during the growth-producing phase of your investment life, you can reinvest dividend payments from REITs are buy more shares.

Over the long term, REITs have produced year-to-year returns that are very competitive with other investments. Annual returns have ranged from 5% up to 16% in recent years. So, you can have a good, solid investment with good annual returns in addition to the dividend payments that you are receiving.

REITs also provide a way to get into property ownership that has unprecedented levels of liquidity. As an investor, you should be intimately familiar with the idea of liquidity. For those who aren't sure what the term means, liquidity basically refers to how easily you can convert an asset into cash, and how quickly you can get in and out of the investment. If you actually own properties, say homes that you rent out, they are far less liquid than a REIT. When it comes to owning a stake in physical property, you are going to have a much harder time getting in and out of your ownership stake. If you don't have cash, you are going to have to apply for a loan to acquire the property. If you want to get out of a property, it might take weeks or months to sell the property on the market, and you might not get the price you wanted.

In contrast, REITs, trading on the stock exchange, allow you to get in and out of investments practically at will. It's no different than buying and selling shares of stock. In addition, you can invest as little or as much at a time as you like. You aren't going to need $250k in cash or be put in a position where you have to get a loan. Instead, all you need to start investing is enough money to buy a single share of a REIT. As soon as your trades are executed, you have your ownership stake. So, they are highly liquid, while actually buying property as an individual is not very liquid.

And yet, REITs will give you the same benefits. You will earn a regular income that is derived from rents of various types of properties.

Four Major Types Of REITs

The first type of REIT that we are going to encounter is called a private REIT. Unless you know someone that owns one and they've invited you to invest, for most readers, you are not going to be concerned with private REITs.

The second type of REIT is called a public, non-listed REIT. This is a public company that is not listed on public stock exchanges. So, you are probably not going to be investing in this type of REIT either.

Next, we have an mREIT. This is a mortgage REIT, which is exactly what it says – it's a company that provides real estate financing. They may also provide mortgage-backed securities.

The final major type of REIT is an equity REIT. An equity REIT is a REIT that owns income-producing real estate or physical assets, and it is publicly traded on a major stock exchange.

As an investor, you can invest in equity REITs and mortgage REITs. Since you can also invest in mortgage REITs by buying shares on a public exchange, you might also think in terms of the type of REIT rather than the definition of equity, in the respect that an equity REIT has equity or an ownership stake in property, but a mortgage REIT doesn't have an ownership stake in properties.

Types Of Equity REITs

There are many, many different types of equity REITs. Let's take a brief look at some of the different ways that you can invest in REITs and build up a very diverse set of ownership stakes in properties.

Retail

Many REITs own retail properties. Even within this class of REITs, there is a lot of variety. For example, many REITs own shopping malls. Others own strip malls or grocery stores. As an owner of a retail-oriented REIT, you will be receiving income through dividend payments that are derived from the rents that tenants of all of these facilities are paying, month-in and month-out.

Industrial

Anything that can be rented out can be owned by a REIT. This means that you can invest in REITs that own industrial facilities. These can include companies that own large manufacturing facilities, or infrastructure related to industrial activities.

Data Centers

Going forward into the new, increasingly computerized world, REITs that own data centers make very good investments. This area of REIT investing is relatively new and likely to see explosive growth in the coming years. Data centers can host cloud computing facilities, and with the growth of machine learning and big data, demand for data centers is likely to increase massively in the coming years. You can get in on the ground floor of this demand by investing in REITs that own data centers.

Communication Infrastructure

As we alluded to earlier, many REITs own some unconventional, but physical assets. This includes communication infrastructure. Specifically, many REITs own cell phone towers. Like data center REITs, those that own cell phone towers can be thought of as REITs of the future. Although this market has matured as nearly everyone has a cell phone these days, the fact remains that cell phone use is not something that is going to go away anytime soon. This means that REITs that own cell phone towers will continue to be good, reliable, and long-term investments.

Office Space

Many REITs own office buildings, which can be fairly lucrative as far as providing regular rent payments. Of course, this type of commercial real estate can be somewhat sensitive to the economy, and during large economic downturns, your fortunes might go down with them. However, as a part of a larger investment portfolio, REITs that own commercial office space can be a good addition.

Residential

One of the outgrowths of the 2008 financial crash was that rates of homeownership took a nosedive. But people have to live somewhere, and rentals of single-family homes have increased significantly.

Like commercial office rentals, this is something that is going to fluctuate up and down with economic fortunes, but it's something that will never go away since everyone needs a place to live. Since the housing crisis, many large investment companies have become involved in the ownership of large numbers of single-family homes. You can take advantage of this trend and earn a regular income from the rents.

Healthcare

Healthcare represents an exciting opportunity for REIT investing. Many people are not aware of this, but many medical facilities are rented. This includes everything from large hospitals to nursing homes. With an aging population, this provides a great opportunity for investment, since the usage of these facilities and growth is not only stable and reliable, it is only going to increase as time goes on.

Self-Storage

Another interesting type of REIT is one where you own self-storage facilities. This is probably not something where you want to put ALL of your money but investing in a REIT that owns self-storage facilities can help you diversify your investments.

Timberlands

This is another obscure investment, but you can invest in REITs that own property with trees that are harvested for timber.

Hotels, Lodging, and Resorts

The final class of REITs that can be a great addition to any investment portfolio are those that specialize in hotel, motel, and lodging. This may surprise many readers, but many major hotel chains actually rent their properties. Some of the renters include big hotel chains like Marriot and Holiday Inn. As you might imagine, REITs that own these properties can be good investments. Likes some of the other types of REITs, this sector can be sensitive to economic ups and downs, but as a part of a diversified portfolio, they can make good investments that pay high yields.

Resources to Research REITs

There are many online resources that you can use to do research on various REITs. The first step is to visit reit.com, a website run by industry associations where you can learn about REITs in detail. You can learn about REIT index funds and gather information on the past performance of REITs.

To find individual REITs to invest in on the stock market, you can visit suredividend.com, which maintains a large list of REITs that are traded on public stock exchanges. Once you become familiar with the tickers used for various REITs and what the companies invest in, you can look them up on

Yahoo Finance or on your own stock brokerage to get information about yields, historical returns, and current share trading prices.

Top REIT Yields

REITs make a solid addition to any investor who is interested in building a diverse portfolio of investments that pays dividends. In this section, we are going to draw your attention to a few of the REITs that pay the highest yields.

- Washington Prime Group Inc: Paying an astoundingly high yield of 22%, Washington Prime Group invests in shopping centers. The stock ticker is WPG. Shares are only $4.45.
- Anworth Mortgage Investment Co.: This is a mortgage real estate investment trust, that takes an unconventional approach. They borrow funds that are then invested in mortgage-backed securities. They pay a 14%

yield, and shares are trading at about $3.50. The ticker is ANH.

- ARMOUR Residential REIT: This REIT has a yield of 13%, which is still very high and is trading at $16 a share. The ticker is ARR.

- Two Harbors Investment Corp: This is another REIT that invests in residential mortgage-backed securities. They have a yield of 13%, and shares are trading at around $13 a share. The ticker is TWO.

As you can see, there are REITs available that have very high yields as compared to stocks, and the share prices are relatively low. Of course, more investigation is recommended before you start investing in any individual REIT. You will want to find out how long it has been in business, how the stock price has varied over time, and how consistent the company has been in maintaining yields and paying dividends. As a part of your REIT investing, you are going to want to invest in a diverse selection of REITs, meaning that in addition to investing in more than one company, you invest in REITs that invest in different types of properties.

Master Limited Partnerships

The next type of company that we are going to look at is called a master limited partnership, or MLP. A master limited partnership is a specific type of business structure that is often used with energy companies. Although real estate and financial companies can be MLPs, the vast majority of them are associated with oil and natural gas operations. The structure of an MLP as a business makes this a particularly lucrative investment that has many tax benefits. From the name, you see that the company is a limited partnership, so it is not a corporation. As an investor, you become a limited partner in the company. These companies have a general partner that runs company operations, but like REITs, they are required by law to distribute 90% of their profits to investors.

Oil and natural gas companies can be divided into three different types, upstream, midstream, and downstream. Upstream companies are involved in the initial stages of energy production. They can be involved in exploration and drilling activities, for example. Downstream companies are those that deal in operations that are closer to the public that uses end products. This can include oil and gas refining activities all the way to the point of sale to the public. Midstream companies are typically involved in transportation and storage of oil and natural gas. Of course, some of the world's largest oil companies like Exxon can be involved in all types of activities.

Master limited partnerships are energy companies that are concentrated in midstream activities. These companies may own oil pipelines, storage facilities, or port facilities. They might be involved in truck or rail transport of oil or natural gas from one location to another. Some are involved in multiple activities; for example, AmeriGas is a natural gas company that is involved in the storage and transport of natural gas products like propane, including delivery to the end consumer.

Advantages of MLPs

An MLP is a publicly traded company on a major stock exchange. As we saw with REITs, this can create an interesting mix of advantages for the investor. The first thing to consider is that a company that has a structure of a partnership is generally not something you think about when you consider the term liquidity. First of all, partnerships tend to be private companies, so finding one that you could invest in is something that might take some work. You might have to have a direct family member with a partnership to typically get involved in that kind of business. So, the truth about partnerships is that they are illiquid.

But one of the benefits of a partnership is that they pass on the expenses of the business to the investors. This can really help reduce tax liabilities. Of course, since partnerships tend to be private businesses, finding one to invest in can be problematic, and if you are able to get invested in one, you might find that it's impossible or difficult to get out of the investment if you want to.

On the other hand, publicly traded companies are very liquid. Well, at least the investments in them are. This is one of the beauties of the stock exchange; you can get in and out of an investment in a company practically in real-time if you want to. So, it's easy to find companies to invest in, and it's easy to sell your investments and convert them into cash. This is one of the draws of the stock market.

MLPs combine the best of both worlds while getting rid of the downsides. MLPs are publicly traded, and therefore investing in MLPs is very easy to do. Since they are traded on major stock exchanges, this means that your investments in MLPs are very liquid. But since they are pass-through partnerships and not corporations, you get the tax advantages of being in a partnership. And this includes being able to deduct the depreciation that the company has on all this equipment like oil storage tanks that we've been talking about. That depreciation is passed on directly to you the investor, and you are able to use it on your taxes. As a result, many investors in MLPs pay little to no income tax on the dividend income that they receive from these companies. The tax advantages, coupled with the high yields many MLPs pay, make them highly coveted dividend investments.

The first MLP was formed in 1981, and soon after, many oil and gas companies changed their business structure to this format. By being able to be traded on major stock exchanges, this gives these companies access to a lot of extra capital they otherwise would not have access to. Although most MLPs today are energy companies, some other forms of business can adopt the MLP structure, including finance, real estate, and hospitality companies, among others.

An MLP has a general partner. In the case of an MLP, the general partners actually run the business. The general partner is not a person per se; often it can be another company. But the general partner runs the day-to-day operations of the business and gets paid a management fee for doing so. Limited partners in the MLP are the investors that buy stock in the company.

As we've mentioned, most MLPs that you are going to come across are midstream energy companies. However, there are also upstream oil and natural gas companies and mineral operations that are run as publicly traded MLPs. Many midstream operators that you can invest in will include storage companies, oil tankers, gas carriers, transport companies that move oil and gas from one place to another, and port facilities. Some MLPs can be involved in activities like oil and gas refining and wholesale distribution.

Another type of MLP that you might come across is a coal mining company, or their arch-nemesis in today's world, renewable energy companies. Some MLPs are involved in finance, such as private equity companies.

Although many different types of businesses can and do adopt the MLP structure, it is estimated that at least 80% of the companies that are MLPs are oil and natural gas companies, and about 9 out of 10 of those companies are midstream oil and natural gas companies.

When you trade shares of MLPs, you are not going to notice anything special. You will go through your brokerage and buy shares in an MLP on the stock market. However, technically speaking, you are not buying shares of stock in the company. Since an MLP is not a corporation, it does not issue stock. Instead, they issue what are called units. And technically speaking, if you own units in an MLP, you are not a shareholder or a stockholder, you are a unitholder.

Also, the payments issued by these companies, although we can treat them as dividends, are not considered to be dividends. Once again, this is a concept that is limited to corporations. Although the payments are essentially dividends in practice, they are considered to be cash distributions.

Things to Look for in MLPs

The first thing to consider with an MLP is the specific kind of business that the company is engaged in. Generally speaking, despite rumblings about a green new deal and electric cars, practicality, and the energy density advantage of "fossil fuels" pretty much guarantees that these industries are going to be around for a very long time, and they are going to have very good financial fortunes for some time. So, if you are worried about solar making these companies obsolete, that is not something you should probably spend your energy worrying too much about.

So, from here, you can look into the company fundamentals just like you would with any other investment. These are publicly traded companies on the major stock exchanges. That means they are going to be subject to the same regulations that any corporation that is traded on the major stock exchanges is subject to. As such, they have their audited financial statements available for you to examine. You can look at their cash flow and earnings, and you can track the history of the business along with its share price and "dividend" payments. Something to note about MLPs is that net income is not considered a reliable indicator of the earnings and cash flow of the company.

Therefore, you will want to look at a measure called EBITDA that will help you get a more accurate picture of the company's cash flow. This means earnings before interest, tax, depreciation, and amortization. Since you get to deduct depreciation from your taxes, this will help you get a more accurate estimate of what the net income of the company really is.

You will also want to pay attention to the debt loads of the company. This is the same thing to look at as you would with a corporation when it comes to debt interfering with a company's ability to pay dividends. However, MLPs seem to be more sensitive to the cash flow problems that can arise when a company takes on too much debt. So, if you see an MLP that you are interested in is carrying a lot of debt, you have to have some concern about their ability to make the cash distribution payments or continue them in the future.

Reduced Tax Liability

I always say that one of the advantages of the rich is they know all the tricks. One of the tricks that you are learning about now that can help boost your real standard of living is the ability to take advantage of the deductions of an MLP to reduce your own taxes. As a partner of the company, the deductions the company takes are passed onto you and you are able to use them on your own taxes as if you had joined your own brother or a friend in forming a partnership to run a business. This can substantially reduce your tax liability in many cases.

Watch out for Retirement Accounts

If you are going to invest in MLPs, you don't want to do so through a retirement account like an IRA. Instead, just buy the shares individually through your broker. The reason is that when there is another layer as in an individual retirement account or a 401k, the account itself becomes the "limited partner" in the business. This can cause problems for you taxwise. Instead of dealing with those hassles, and to take advantage of the tax breaks that are available, just buy the shares without going through an IRA to do it.

Of course, MLPs are available through mutual funds and exchange-traded funds as well. You can use this approach to invest in MLPs and get around the tax headaches that could be involved in investing in these types of companies through a 401k or an IRA. In other words, if you want to invest directly in MLPs, do it through your broker, and do it in a regular brokerage account and not through any retirement account. This means buying shares directly on the stock market. On the other hand, if you want to invest in MLPs but would prefer to keep things in a 401k or an IRA, then you should invest in mutual funds or exchange-traded funds that have holdings in MLPs.

Economic Factors Impacting MLPs

Most readers are probably acutely aware of the economic impacts that can take their toll on MLPs. Oil and natural gas have been in boom times in recent years, but many things can have a major impact on oil and gas prices, and if you start investing a lot in these companies, you'll be tying yourself to that sector of the economy.

There are a large number of things that could impact the value of your investments. These include everything from day-to-day fluctuations in oil and natural gas prices to wars, and to political events, among other things.

Note that some political candidates are talking about banning fracking and moving on to "green" energy technologies. It is unlikely that the latter will move ahead all that much, simply due to the practical power of oil and natural gas as energy sources. However, the environment for midstream oil and gas companies can be made much more hostile than it is now, by politicians. So, you have to be aware of these possibilities, and factor that into your investment decisions.

Oil and natural gas prices can be very volatile, even without major political upheavals. Therefore, this is something that you are going to have to figure into your investments. And it's a good reason to have a generally diversified portfolio. As attractive as investing in MLPs can be, you certainly don't want to have an investment portfolio that only consists of MLPs.

If you have a diversified portfolio of which they are only a part, then when there are oil and gas shocks, you can just wait them out. Remember that the economy and sectors like this will experience boom and bust times and cycles.

It can be argued that the magnitude and frequency of boom and bust are stronger in the energy sector than it is anywhere else. But the fact remains, that at least for now, people need oil and gas, and society needs it to keep functioning. So, investments in oil and gas are on average, going to be good investments.

High Yields

The yields paid out by many MLPs, like REITs, are quite high, relatively speaking. So, in addition to the tax advantages that you can get with MLPs, you will be able to take advantage of fantastically high yields as compared to those typically offered by regular corporations. Dividend payments can be quite high in absolute terms, and many companies have modest share prices as well. This makes it easier to acquire the number of shares you would need to reach a given level of income from your cash flow payments, which play the role of dividends in this case.

Tax Forms

Investors in an MLP will receive a K-1 form each year that will state your shares of profit and loss that are associated with the company.

Business Development Companies

The final unusual type of business that we are going to look at for income investing is called a Business Development Company or BDC. This type of company has a similar structure to those used by the other types of companies we have discussed, with the important similarity being that they will pay most of their profits out (once again it will be required to be at least 90%) to investors.

Business development companies tend to be financing companies that will either fund private businesses, take equity stakes in businesses, or provide financing to distressed companies.

Typically, these types of companies target the financial needs of smaller businesses that are not able to get funding elsewhere. A BDC can take an investment stake in a small business, and therefore own stock in the company, or it can provide loans and therefore hold debt. If a BDC is issuing loans to small businesses, although there is a risk that some of these businesses are going to default, as an investor you can take advantage of this by receiving a share of the loan payments that are going to be made to the BDC as the companies it has lent funds to pay their loans back.

A BDC is treated as a "regulated investment company" by the IRS. The details don't really concern us as dividend investors, the important fact to note is that once again this is a type of company structure that requires them to pass on 90% of their taxable income to investors.
Like a REIT or MLP, investors benefit from the fact that these companies don't have to pay corporate taxes. This will help boost your earnings, and it makes higher yields possible since once again, there is no double taxation in this case.
They simply pass on their earnings to investors, who are then required to pay the tax on their earnings.

One downside, however, when it comes to income from a BDC is that although you can think of this income as being distributed as dividends, it cannot be used as qualified dividends, and its paid out as and treated as regular income.

So, you will be paying ordinary income tax on any payments you receive from a BDC. However, if the BDC earns money in the form of capital gains that are then passed on to investors, this income can be taxed at the more favorable capital gains tax rates, if they are long-term capital gains.

Like REITs and MLPs, BDCs are traded on the major stock exchanges. Despite their unusual business structure, many of these companies are quite large in scale. One of the most well-known BDCs is Apollo Investment. This company pays a very high 14% yield.

Typically, high yields are paid when risk is higher, and this is definitely true for BDCs. Due to the nature of the business, BDCs are always facing the risk of default from their customers, which are often distressed small businesses. Of course, many small businesses fail, and this is something that can put the revenue from BDCs at risk.

In fact, the average yield for business development companies is above 9%. But always use caution when you see higher yields. This does not mean that you shouldn't invest in companies paying high yields; it simply means that you need to do your due diligence in each case.

Since BDCs are involved strictly in financial operations, and a large part of their business is involved in issuing credits to small businesses, BDCs are subject to interest rate risk.

In today's environment, that might not be too important, since we are in what is probably the lowest interest rate environment there has ever been in history. Second, at least for now, the Federal Reserve seems pretty unwilling to raise interest rates by very much.

In any case, when interest rates do rise, this could have a material impact on business development companies. Small businesses may be less inclined to borrow funds from these companies if interest rates are rising.

Another way that BDCs can get into trouble is by using leverage themselves. By borrowing money to fund their operations, BDCs are able to magnify their returns and pass on those magnified returns on to their investors in the form of profits. Of course, this is another way that interest rate risk can impact business development companies.

Just like with other types of investments, if you are interested in BDCs but don't want to take the risk of investing in them directly, you can find mutual funds and exchange-traded funds that will help you to invest in a wide array of BDCs. This can help you to reduce your risk since you will be investing in funds that will, in turn, be investing in a large number of these companies so that you don't have to take the risk of putting a large amount of your own capital in a BDC.

ETFs For REITs, MLPs, And BDCs

As we discussed, there are reasons to invest in either mutual funds or exchange-traded funds when considering some of these unconventional investments. It will help to dilute your risk, as well as giving you exposure without having to deal with extra tax implications.

Many companies, including major investment houses, offer ETFs that invest in REITs, for example. These include the SPDR Dow Jones REIT ETF (RWR), the Schwab REIT ETF (SCHH), and the Vanguard Real Estate ETF (VNQ). The yields of these funds are 3.2%, 2.69%, and 3.12%. After all the high yields we've been talking about, these kinds of yields might make you fall flat. Remember the trade-off; high yields are a signal of higher levels of risk. If your overall portfolio is highly diversified, in my opinion, it can't hurt to have some very high yield investments in REITs as a part of your portfolio.

But if you personally have a lower risk tolerance, then you know you can get exposure to real estate by investing in funds like these, and still earn what would be a halfway decent yield if we were talking about investments in ordinary stocks.

Likewise, there are many ETFs that invest in MLPs that you can consider. The First Trust North American Energy Infrastructure Fund (EMLP) pays a yield of 3.8%, with a fairly dramatic 20% year-to-date return. If you are looking for an ETF with high yields, consider the Alerian MLP ETF, which has a yield of 8.43%, a share price of $8.43, with a modest year-to-date return of 5.45%.

Another good option in the MLP space is the Global X MLP and Energy Infrastructure ETF, which is trading at just $12 a share. This fund has enjoyed a year to date return of 14% and offers a yield of 5.78%, so this fund serves as a kind of middle ground.

Several banking companies like JP Morgan and Wells Fargo offer ETFs that track business development companies. Yields for these funds are often in the 8-9% range, close to the industry average. So, it's possible to get the average yield for the sector but with the diversified exposure that an exchange-traded fund can provide.

Chapter 9: Solid Annual Returns Through Indirect Bond Investing

Although bond investing is not dividends, by using ETFs we can essentially convert bonds into stocks and get a dividend payment. This can be incorporated with everything that we have discussed so far, to further diversify your dividend investment portfolio. And by investing in ETFs that hold bonds, you can enjoy solid annual returns in addition to the income payments that you would get from the bonds themselves. Investing in bonds as an individual can also be a more difficult and complicated process. By using exchange-traded funds, you can keep things simple by investing what is from your perspective, just another stock.

What Is A Bond?

For those readers who are not familiar with bonds, a bond is a form of a loan. An issuing entity, which could be a government or a corporation, will issue bonds, which in short means they are offering you the chance to make them a loan. Your investment is buying the bond which gives the company or government entity a loan in cash. In return for making the loan, the issuing entity will pay you interest for the lifetime of the bond, until it expires.

Many people are familiar with the many different bonds that are issued by the U.S. government. These include treasury notes, bills, and bonds, along with US Savings Bonds. The U.S. government also issues Savings Bonds.

For historical reasons, the interest payment made on a bond is sometimes referred to as the coupon. This refers to the old days when you would tear a coupon off your bond certificate and take it down to receive your payment. Of course, today this is all done electronically by computer, but you might hear the term coupon. You may also hear par value, which refers to the face value of the bond.

State, county, and city governments also issue bonds that are called municipal bonds. These types of bonds have interest payments that are exempt from federal income tax, and as such, they have been a favored method used by the wealthy to avoid paying federal income tax. When income tax rates in the United States were in the 70-90% range, the wealthy moved a lot of their money into "munis" to avoid paying the high tax rates.

Corporations also issue bonds as another way of raising funding. Most large corporations issue bonds to one degree or another. Even very healthy companies like Apple issue bonds and take on debt.

Companies that have a bad credit history are given bad ratings, and since they have had past troubles paying their debts back, they are known as "junk bonds." Despite the reputation they have gained due to past failures to pay back the principal, they are still attracting investors because of the high-interest rates they offer.

Bonds are traded on secondary markets, as you would expect. Prices of bonds fluctuate in an inverse relationship to interest rates. If interest rates are going down, that means that bonds that were issued in the past, which therefore will pay higher interest rates, gain value. That is because investors want to buy them to get the higher interest rate payments. So, they bid up the prices on the secondary markets.

On the other hand, if interest rates rise, that makes newly issued bonds more valuable, and bonds that were issued in the past when interest rates were lower less desirable. So, in that case, bond prices are going to fall.

It is these fluctuations that can make the share prices of exchange-traded funds that own bonds go up and down. It is a good idea to understand why things are happening when you are investing. If interest rates rise in the future, then bond prices are going to drop across the board. On the other hand, if interest rates are dropped again in an attempt to goose the economy, that is going to mean that bond prices will rise.

This phenomenon can also impact individual bonds. If a company's credit rating goes bad, when it issues new bonds, the prices of existing bonds on the market will drop, because investors could receive higher interest payments from the newly issued bonds, provided they are willing to take the risk on investing with a company that has defaulted in the past.

Bonds In ETFs

For our purposes, we are not going to be interested in direct investments in bonds. Instead, we want to explore using bonds as a part of our dividend income strategy. As we mentioned in the opening passage of the chapter, the way that we can accomplish this is by investing in exchange-traded funds that have ownership stakes in bonds. There is a wide range of these funds to choose from, and you can find funds that invest in virtually every type of bond.

Bond ETFs are going to work in a similar fashion to dividend ETFs. Begin by imaging a bond fund that holds many different bonds. As they pay interest, the fund manager is going to collect all the interest payments. These will then be divided by the total number of shares in the fund, to get an overall payment, which his then going to be distributed to investors. The interest payments are paid to investors in the form of a dividend.

Remember that even though we are talking about bonds, as an investor in the ETF you own stock.

One of the nice things about bond ETFs is that they are going to pay the interest collected from the bonds as a monthly dividend. The fund may also generate capital gains, as it sells bonds to earn a profit. Capital gains in bond exchange-traded funds are paid to investors in the form of an annual dividend.

Bond ETFs To Invest In

One of the most popular bond funds is JNK, a bond exchange-traded fund that invests in poor credit corporate bonds – in other words, junk bonds. The fund has a 5.53% yield and a year-to-date return of 13%.

LQD is the iShares investment-grade bond fund. Investment-grade bonds are corporate bonds issued by companies with better credit. Since the companies have good credit, the downside for the investor in an ETF is that they pay lower yields. When we are talking about ETFs, higher yields may be worth the risk because you are not going to have much exposure to one single company that might go bad when paying its debts.

There are bond funds for government bonds of all types, and some bond funds, like FLDR, mix government bonds and corporate bonds into the same exchange-traded fund. SHY is an offering from iShares that invests in 1-3-year US Treasury bonds. Being low-risk investments, Treasury bond funds are going to be funds that have lower yields. That is something to consider when making your selections.

Bond ETFs – Are They Worth It?

The advantage of investing in bonds is that you get your principal back. Well, at least most of the time, since there are many companies that have defaulted on bond payments. Generally speaking, however, bonds are considered "safe" investments that protect your principal while offering regular income in return. Financial advisors tell people that they are getting closer to retirement to protect their existing capital by moving more of it out of stocks and into bonds. Here, we are not talking about investing directly in bonds, however, so the risks are not exactly the same. Whether you decide to include bonds in your overall investment plan when you are looking to build a portfolio designed for dividend income is something that is up to you, but it is clear that exchange-traded funds, which essentially convert bonds into stock investments that pay monthly dividends, can definitely be something to add on to your overall investment plan. It's another way to help make your investments more diverse. Moreover, investments in bonds can also provide some security during stock market crashes and downturns. A rule of thumb is that when the stock market goes down, bond markets go up and vice versa. If you have some holdings in ETFs that track bonds, you are going to be able to take advantage of some of the protection that this offers.

So, in the opinion of this author, a portion of your portfolio should be devoted to bond ETFs. I would advise against direct investments in bonds themselves, since you can enjoy all the benefits that bonds have to offer in diversified holdings using ETFs, and you don't really have to learn much extra. Fundamental analysis, in this case, is going to involve tracking the overall economy and monitoring interest rate changes. So, if you invest in bonds, you'll be paying a lot more attention to federal reserve meetings and announcements.

Some investors may decide they want to invest in bonds themselves, directly. This is a bit of an extra hassle. Bonds are not traded in markets the way stocks are, and if you want to buy bonds, you are going to have to do it "over the counter." Probably the easiest way to invest in bonds directly is by investing in U.S. government bonds. One of the favorite investments for protecting capital is TIPS, which are inflation-protected Treasuries offered by the US government. Therefore, if you want to protect capital, that might be an option for you to consider.

Chapter 10: Dealing with Taxes

Of course, when you are receiving regular payments from your investments, the IRS is going to take an interest. In this chapter, we are going to very briefly examine the tax implications of dividend investing.

Capital Gains Taxes

The first thing to note about investing if you are not aware of this is how capital gains are treated. If an investment is held for less than a year, then it is considered a short-term capital gain. The bottom line for a short-term capital gain is that it is taxed as ordinary income.

A long-term capital gain is one that is held for a year or longer. Investments that are held for a year or longer and then are sold for a profit are taxed at the long-term capital gains tax rates. These can be very favorable, and they are not counted as income, so you are not going to be paying social security and Medicare taxes on these funds either.

Qualified Vs. Unqualified Dividends

For dividends, the key question is whether or not they are going to be taxed as qualified or unqualified dividends. This is something that is going to determine whether or not you can take advantage of long-term capital gains tax rates, or whether your dividends are going to be taxed as ordinary income.

The first question to ask for a dividend is who paid it. If a U.S. based corporation paid it, this is in favor of the dividend is qualified. It has to be a corporation – something that we will discuss below. The second thing to consider is how long you have owned the stock. If you have owned the stock for more than 60 days within a 120-day holding period centered on the ex-dividend date, then this is a qualified dividend provided it has also met the first criteria.

If the dividend is qualified, then you can pay the long-term capital gains tax rate on dividend income. If you hold the same stocks for a long time period, this should not be a problem for you, and you will be able to enjoy the lower tax rates that come with dividend income. The purpose of these laws is to encourage long term thinking when it comes to investing.

If your dividends are unqualified, then the income from the dividends will be treated as regular income. As it will be a regular income, you may be liable for FICA taxes on the income as well.

Income From REITs, MLPs, And BDCs

Income from real estate trusts, master limited partnerships, and business development companies are considered regular income. It is not treated as qualified dividend income or long-term capital gains. So, although you will enjoy the high yields that come from these investments, you are also going to be faced with higher rates of taxation as well. Also, keep in mind that you may be liable for social security and Medicare taxes on the income derived from these dividend payments as well.

MLPs offer a benefit that the income from real estate trusts and business development companies does not, in that income from MLPs is going to be passed along with the losses or deductions the company takes on its operations as well, something we discussed in the chapter on these types of investments. In the case of MLPs, this can help to offset the extra taxes that you would otherwise be facing.

Surtaxes

Since Obamacare became law, high-income folks that receive dividend payments may be subject to the Medicare surtax. This will add an additional 3.8% to any tax rate that you owe on income from dividends. This is going to be true whether or not you are facing taxes based on qualified or unqualified dividends. A single taxpayer, you are subject to the Obamacare surtax if you have adjusted gross income of $200,000 or higher. For married joint filers, the surtax kicks in with an adjusted gross income of $250,000 or higher.

Dividend Income Vs. Other Types Of Investment Income

Since long-term investors that get income from U.S. corporations are going to be dealing with qualified dividends, this means that you are going to be enjoying favorable tax rates in the form of the long-term capital gains tax rates. The tax rates are 0% or 15%, depending on your regular income tax rate. For those with a regular income tax rate of 15% or lower, your capital gains tax rate is 0%. For those with an income tax rate of 25% or higher, your capital gains tax rate will be 15%. For other types of investments, you would be facing the prospect of treating your investment income as regular income. So not only would you be facing the prospect of paying regular income tax rates, which are going to be higher, but you would also be having to possibly pay social security and Medicare taxes on the income.

Chapter 11: Top Ten High-Yield Picks for 2020

1. IBM: A long-time blue-chip company that has shown great stock appreciation while continuing to pay solid dividends with a yield of 4.8%.

2. AbbVie: This is a 100-year-old pharmaceutical company that was spun off from Abbott medical. A long-lasting and solid company that pays decent yields.

3. Intel: The semiconductor chip company remains a solid bet. Yields are a more modest 2.5%.

4. Companhia Energetica (CI-G). This energy company pays a 4% yield, with solid annual returns.

5. Spark Energy: A utility company that pays a 6% yield.

6. Carlyle Group: An investment firm that deals with private equity, a solid yield of 7%.

7. Terraform Power: Get in on the green energy revolution and enjoy a 5% yield.

8. Outfront Media: A nice way to diversify your holdings. Has a solid 5% yield.

9. Buckeye Partners: A good MLP involved in midstream oil and gas, 7% yield.

10. Apple: The only FAANG that pays dividends. Still a solid bet.

Conclusion

Thank you for making it through to the end of *Dividend Investing*, let's hope it was informative and able to provide you with all of the tools you need to achieve your goals whatever they may be.

Now is as good as any time to begin your career as a self-directed investor. If you haven't already opened up a brokerage account, you should get on that as soon as possible. It isn't complicated, and once you take that first step, you will begin to reduce any anxiety or hesitation you are feeling about beginning your own investment program.

Remember that you can contribute an amount that works for you. Don't worry about the examples discussed in this book or elsewhere or what other people are doing, invest an amount that is within your budget and your abilities to start investing on a regular basis. Even if you start off only investing $50 a month, the simple fact that you are getting into the habit of running your own investment program is the important thing to focus on. You can always up your contributions later.

I do urge all readers to do their due diligence when it comes to investing. Beginning a process of taking control of your own investments and financial future can be exhilarating but remember that it also comes with responsibility. If you make investments and fail, the fact that you are following a self-directed and independent investment program means that if your investments fail there is nobody to blame but yourself.

But we have provided the tools you need to avoid failure. If you follow a program of diversification and dollar-cost averaging, along with making regular at least monthly contributions, unless there is an overall economic calamity you are not going to fail. But have realistic expectations, as far as understanding the amount of money that you can earn based on the size of your investments and the time horizons that you are going to use when building up your investments.

As you invest, make sure to diversify widely. Don't just pick a few different stocks, also focus on investing in some REITs, MLPs, BDCs, and possibly some bond exchange-traded funds.

Also, be sure to continue your investment education. An education in investing is something that should be a "continued education" that lasts for a lifetime. Keep reading books, listening to radio programs, and watching videos. Follow financial and economic news in publications like the Financial Times and the Wall Street Journal, and you can even devote time to keeping up with news by watching CNBC and Fox Business. When it comes to TV, just avoid getting swept up in the hype. It is also important to avoid falling for the next "big" investment. As a dividend investor, you should be approaching your investments with a mindset of careful, deliberate investing that builds up an account slowly but surely, over time. You are the turtle who wins the race when it comes to investing, ignore all the rabbits (aka day traders, speculators) that you are going to be well ahead of when retirement arrives.

Finally, if you found this book useful in any way, a review on Amazon is highly appreciated!

Reviews are crucial for a book to survive on Amazon. Hence, we as authors heavily depend on them.
So, if you found this book useful in any way, I would be delighted to see a review from you with a simple feedback on what you liked and what could be improved.

Thank you so much for reading to the end of this book, and good luck with your endeavors in the world of dividend investing!